P9-DOG-925

"Simply excellent! A wonderful mix of captivating personal experiences, biblical teaching, and probing structural analysis. Mayfield gently draws us in as she candidly shares her doubts and struggles, and she vigorously challenges us with her powerful summons to see and change systemic injustice. Unless the evangelical world begins to understand the fundamental critique of this book and truly repent and change, we do not deserve to continue to exist. A must-read."

Ron Sider, distinguished professor emeritus of theology, holistic ministry and public policy, Palmer Seminary at Eastern University, author of *Rich Christians in an Age of Hunger*

"In my work with immigrants to the US, I find most came in search of some combination of safety from persecution, opportunity to escape poverty, and freedom from oppression—all motivations consistent with the human flourishing that characterizes God's kingdom. In the US, however, these good desires that define many immigrants' 'American dream' have too often metastasized as we have turned safety, affluence, power, and autonomy into idols to be sought at all costs, even when—sometimes subconsciously—these pursuits have excluded others. D. L. Mayfield's beautifully written and provocative *The Myth of the American Dream* makes a compelling case that God's dream for the world is much grander than our culturally ingrained idols."

Matthew Soerens, coauthor of *Welcoming the Stranger*, US director of church mobilization for World Relief

"Three pages into *The Myth of the American Dream* I was reminded that D. L. Mayfield is an unapologetic truth teller devoted to loving her neighbors. She has a prophetic voice, and like all prophets, she speaks the truth while reminding us God loves us. That is why we are invited not to a life of charity but of solidarity and advocacy with those on the margins. In her book, we learn ethics matter, integrity matters, and we cannot say we love our neighbors while supporting an empire that exploits and discards them. With humility and honesty, she guides our imaginations toward a powerful vision of a life lived according to the economy of God, one of justice and flourishing for all."

Karen González, World Relief, author of *The God Who Sees*

"The American dream, a common developed theology, tucked deep inside the myth of America's founding, saturates every system in America from politics to education to the church. This so-called dream is perhaps the most widespread and deepest held religion in our country. D. L. Mayfield examines the myth and exposes it in wonderful juxtaposition to the real Jesus of the Gospels, who is good news to the poor and disenfranchised. I wish every American, regardless of how much they believe themselves to have separated themselves from the national religion of Americanism, would read *The Myth of the American Dream*. This may be the most important book you read for some time, and it is especially urgent that you read it now!"

Randy Woodley, author and speaker, distinguished professor of faith and culture at Portland Seminary

"D. L. Mayfield is one of our most important contemplative writers. Her meditation on the myths we live and the better story Jesus offers is hearty soul food for all who hunger for justice. Eat this book. And like any good meal, share it with those you love."

Jonathan Wilson-Hartgrove, author of *Revolution of Values*

"This book is most welcome as both a challenge and an inspiration to live out our lives as Christians first and Americans second. The conflation of the US church's spiritual identity with our political identity and the persistent pursuit of affluence, autonomy, safety, and power have become toxic to our followership with Jesus Christ and incapacitated our ability to live out and express to a watching and waiting world what the gospel is all about. This book doesn't just startle us out of our misaligned pursuit of the American dream but also points us to a better way of how we can love God and love our neighbors in tangible ways that demonstrate to a broken world that Jesus indeed calls us to an upside-down kingdom. I'm grateful for D. L.'s ongoing commitment to her neighbors and for her experiences that she weaves into this timely and important book that ultimately points us to a better way of hope, community, and healing."

Jenny Yang, vice president of advocacy and policy, World Relief, coauthor of *Welcoming the Stranger*

"Christians looking for a list of things to do to address privilege, affluence, and white supremacy should not read this book because D. L. Mayfield does not offer pithy, easy answers. This is not a self-help book for dealing with guilt. She offers us her failures and questions, challenges us to consider how our lives and faith have been shaped and misshapen by the myth of the American dream, and invites us to interrogate our beliefs and lives. What a needed invitation."

Kathy Khang, author of *Raise Your Voice*

"D. L. Mayfield is a fierce truth-teller, and *The Myth of the American Dream* is proof of that. This book confronts us with the demons of white supremacy, *our own demons*, and asks what we're going to do about them. This book reminds us that our lives are more than our own and that we are required to ask how to be better partners to one another in community. This is a book the white American church needs right now."

Kaitlin B. Curtice, author of *Glory Happening* and *Native: Identity, Belonging, and Rediscovering God*

"This trenchant Christian critique of American exceptionalism provides an essential, passionate interpretation of the ideals of egalitarianism."

Publishers Weekly, starred review

THE MYTH OF THE AMERICAN DREAM

D. L. MAYFIELD

REFLECTIONS ON AFFLUENCE, AUTONOMY, SAFETY, AND POWER

An imprint of InterVarsity Press
Downers Grove, Illinois

InterVarsity Press
P.O. Box 1400, Downers Grove, IL 60515-1426
ivpress.com
email@ivpress.com

InterVarsity Press® is the book-publishing division of InterVarsity Christian Fellowship/USA®, a movement of students and faculty active on campus at hundreds of universities, colleges, and schools of nursing in the United States of America, and a member movement of the International Fellowship of Evangelical Students. For information about local and regional activities, visit intervarsity.org.

While any stories in this book are true, some names and identifying information may have been changed to protect the privacy of individuals.

Published in association with the Books & Such Literary Management, 52 Mission Circle, Suite 122, PMB 170, Santa Rosa, CA 95409-5370, www.booksandsuch.com.

Cover design and image composite: David Fassett
Interior design: Daniel van Loon
Images: white wall background: © Nadine Westveer / EyeEm / Getty Images
100 dollar bill close-up: © Chee Siong The / EyeEm / Getty Images
100 dollar bill: © Jun / iStock / Getty Images Plus
blank postage stamp: © troyek / E+ / Getty Images
grunge paper texture: © paladin13 / iStock / Getty Images Plus

ISBN 978-0-8308-4598-9 (print)
ISBN 978-0-8308-4824-9 (digital)

Printed in the United States of America ♾

InterVarsity Press is committed to ecological stewardship and to the conservation of natural resources in all our operations. This book was printed using sustainably sourced paper.

Library of Congress Cataloging-in-Publication Data
Names: Mayfield, Danielle L., author.
Title: The myth of the American dream : reflections on affluence, autonomy, safety, and power / D.L. Mayfield.
Description: Downers Grove, Illinois : InterVarsity Press, [2020] | Includes bibliographical references.
Identifiers: LCCN 2019059215 (print) | LCCN 2019059216 (ebook) | ISBN 9780830845989 (hardcover) | ISBN 9780830848249 (ebook)
Subjects: LCSH: Christian life. | Christianity and culture—United States. | American dream—Religious aspects—Christianity.
Classification: LCC BV4501.3 .M318 2020 (print) | LCC BV4501.3 (ebook) | DDC 261.0973—dc23
LC record available at https://lccn.loc.gov/2019059215
LC ebook record available at https://lccn.loc.gov/2019059216

P 22 21 20 19 18 17 16 15 14 13 12 11 10 9 8 7 6 5 4 3 2 1
Y 38 37 36 35 34 33 32 31 30 29 28 27 26 25 24 23 22 21 20

TO MY NEIGHBORS

CONTENTS

INTRODUCTION ✶ THE MYTH OF THE AMERICAN DREAM

For the time is coming when people will not endure sound teaching, but having itching ears they will accumulate for themselves teachers to suit their own passions, and will turn away from listening to the truth and wander off into myths.

2 TIMOTHY 4:3-4

I AM ON A WALK IN MY NEIGHBORHOOD in January. The air is cold, the ground is wet, but the sun breaks out for a few moments. I see sidewalks on a side street and am struck by the green moss growing on them. It reminds me of old growth; the moss has been there for a long time, and it will remain until whatever it is affixed to crumbles into dust. Other things I see on my walk: a used diaper, a pile of orange-colored vomit, the father of my daughter's schoolmate driving away in a small red car. Two For Sale signs on houses. Hot sauce packets scattered on the ground. Trees bare and stretching to the sky.

Yet the moss hums with a vibrancy, it clings and covers that which remains. My son calls it fairy carpet because I taught him to say this. I am working on seeing little bits of magic where I can. I teach my children, and they teach me, our sight lines going to such different places. Look up, look down. I am learning to look at the ground again, to marvel at the good and the bad equally. I am learning to let the place teach me. This is probably as zen as I will ever get: meditating on bright green moss on a cold January day. This is how I am paying attention today.

I used to prayer walk, bold as brass, longing to witness to others. Now I walk the streets that make up my underresourced, glorious neighborhood, and I try to lean into in the gift of *being* a witness to the good and the bad of the world, to articulating the reality of my neighbors, to God's presence and God's absence. I guess this means I've undergone a conversion of sorts. I suppose this means I am probably trying to convert you too.

★ ★ ★

Here's the story of one of my many conversions: when I was young and convinced the world was mine to save, I started volunteering with Somali Bantu refugees. They had survived the worst the world had to offer only to come to my city and suffer in new and different ways. This shocked me, as it would shock most people who have been sheltered from the realities of the world. I tried to be strong, I tried not to flinch as every one of my most dearly held beliefs about the goodness of God and the goodness of my country wilted in front of me as I started to see life through the eyes of the refugees of the world.

One day I went into the apartment of a Somali Bantu family. There, on the counter, was a stack of bills. No one in the family could read in any language, and translators were few and far between. They asked me to read the bills, and I thumbed through the stack, the costs of the American Dream piling up in that apartment with just a few curtains hung up for decorations, a pot of stew bubbling on the stove. One of the envelopes contained a staggering sum, the cost of the plane rides from the refugee camp in Kenya to the United States for this family of six. The bill was for thousands of dollars.

I held it in my hands, my fingers burning. I hadn't realized that refugees have to pay back the very tickets that supposedly mark their lucky chance to become a part of the dream. What should I tell my new friends? That they were already in debt, already in a hole that I saw no clear path out of? Looking at the faces smiling expectantly back at me, I felt a great chasm grow in my chest as I realized how wide the gap was between how I wish the world was and how it actually was.

When I was young, it was so simple. I thought God was good. I thought God rewarded those who obeyed the rules. I thought my good news was accessible to everyone if only they had the ears to listen. I thought my country was a place where hard work was rewarded on a level playing field, no matter where you came from. Luckily, my life was complicated in beautiful ways that scraped at my very soul. I was plunged into a situation where I was confronted with my privilege and there was no way to wriggle out of it. Volunteering with, working with, and eventually living alongside people who had experienced forced migration help to shatter the unspoken norms I had built up in my mind—what I call the myth of the American Dream, but which can also be called empire or dominant culture ideology.

I slowly realized I did not have a worldview or an ethical framework that accounted for realities different from my own. I was unable to solve the problems of my new friends with my correct doctrine, a Protestant work ethic, and the belief that I was at the tail end of a long line of people who had perfected the art of getting everything right about how to be a human. While the bills and stories and heartbreaks piled up in the lives of people around me, I had to recognize that there were larger forces at play that negatively affected people in my own city, country, and the world—and these systems seemed to harm people in particular who were not White, middle-class evangelicals like me.

This has not been an easy conversion, and I am still in the throes of it. White evangelicals like myself are uniquely unprepared to engage in issues from an institutional or systemic perspective.[1] Our belief in individualism (especially free-will individualism, where each person is accountable to God for their own choices) can lead to the denial, dismissal, or erasure of larger problems or one's responsibility to them. Many White evangelicals grow up believing sin (including large issues like racism, sexism, and economic exploitation) to be a *heart* issue, due to our original sin nature, solved by a personal relationship with Jesus.[2]

If you had asked me what Jesus came to do, growing up the daughter of a pastor I would have said he came to die and pay the price for the sins of those who believe in him. A few years ago I realized something: that is not actually how Jesus defined his own life and work. Instead, Luke 4 tells us that when he wanted to announce his ministry, he went to the synagogue in his hometown and read a striking passage of Scripture. He went straight to the heart of the religiously upright, those who knew all the right answers and quoted their own wild prophets right back to them.

The book of Isaiah is chock full of indictments against the oppressive forces of its day, railing against what happens when the people of God forgot how to obey, how they started to ignore and forget the poor. So it is no surprise that Jesus used the book of Isaiah to lay the groundwork of his movement. And this is what he announced to that crowd:

> The Spirit of the Lord is upon me,
> because he has anointed me
> to bring good news to the poor.
> He has sent me to proclaim release for the captives
> and recovery of sight to the blind,
> to let the oppressed go free,
> to proclaim the year of the Lord's favor. (Luke 4:18-19 NRSV)

Perhaps I had never paid attention to this passage because I had never been truly poor or in prison; I was neither blind nor very oppressed. But now, thanks to my relationships with refugees, I did know people who fit these categories, and I was desperate for a God who was good news for them. The more I read this passage, the more I studied who Jesus was drawn to and who was drawn to him, the more it became clear: this wasn't just Jesus announcing what he had come to do. This was Jesus providing a road map for where we would always find him at work in the world. And what did it mean that for most of my life I had been headed in the opposite direction?

★ ★ ★

The Sufi poet Hafiz wrote, "Slipping on my shoes, boiling water, toasting bread, buttering the sky: that should be enough contact with God in one day to make anyone crazy."[3]

There's a progression here that I identify with. Waking up to the world, slowly, until you realize that everything is upended. Being faithful to swing your legs over the side of the bed, to put on the slippers. To boil the water for the coffee. And the next minute you find yourself waving your butter knife to the sky—perhaps in anger, perhaps in frustration, perhaps in gratitude. The exact reason isn't important. But buttering the sky is a way we reach out to God when the normal routines of our life are no longer enough.

For many of us, our lives have been carefully designed to follow certain values: life, liberty, and the pursuit of happiness, perhaps. When I started to meditate on Luke 4, on taking Jesus at his word that this is the work he came to do, my own unspoken values started to shimmer to the surface. I began by asking questions: What is the opposite of poor? Of captivity, blindness, oppression? As I meditated on this question, the answers surprised me. The answers, it turned out, were the defining values of my life, the ones I was perpetually striving for, all in the name of a "good" life.

Affluence, autonomy, safety, and power. Four concrete values that bled into each other and seeped into my bones, affecting the decisions I made every day, from the tiniest to the monumental. I feel drawn to pursue these values with little to no self-interrogation: of course, I want a good house in a good neighborhood, a stable job, the ability to provide for myself and my family, the best education possible for our kids, a life of ease and comfort, the ability to keep death and pain at bay, the opportunity to lead and to be at the top of the hierarchy, to be seen as an expert and accomplished, to take what I am owed by my virtue and hard work.

Fighting for, hoarding, colonizing, and grasping after each of these values was something so ingrained in me that I didn't recognize how powerful these desires had become or how they had oriented me in the opposite direction to Jesus. And I do mean opposite: when people of privilege pursue affluence, autonomy, safety, and power above everything else, not only do they miss out on the liberating and restorative work of Jesus, but they participate in greater inequality, segregation, and suffering for the most marginalized people in their community. When people of means pursue what is best for them and their own in an unequal society, their actions inevitably harm the common good. People like myself end up disobeying the central commandment of Jesus—to love God and to love our neighbors as ourselves—all in the name of pursuing a dream life for ourselves.

★ ★ ★

The myth of the American Dream comes in many forms, but its most basic iteration goes like this: anyone can make something of themselves if only they try hard enough. This myth is a double-edged sword. If the systems and structures that shape your world have worked for you, then you will believe this idea; it will strengthen your worldview and give you confidence that you've done something right, that you're being rewarded for a job well done. And if other people experience it differently—say, if they are unable to find a job that pays a living wage or get access to education or secure a loan to buy a house—then something must be wrong with them, not the system. The myth of the American Dream not only baptizes the actions and desires of the privileged but also places the blame of inequality on those who are already disadvantaged, instead of turning the focus on changing the unjust systems.

In this book I will consider the narratives lying beneath the surface of so many easy answers that both American culture and American evangelicalism have given to the problem of suffering in an unequal and unjust world. I will attempt to show what it has been like to learn to practice the discipline of lament and how I am being changed by my relationship to people who are exiles from the American Dream—those who have no way to win or who have been excluded from the very beginning. I will share how I have tried, and failed and keep trying to live in opposition to what I've been told (even by the church) is best for me. The more I try to follow Jesus, the more I realize that if the gospel isn't good news for the poor, the imprisoned, the broken-hearted, and the oppressed, then it isn't good news for me either.

This is a book about paying attention. It's about being fully alive, not just to the glories of electric green moss stubbornly growing between the cracks of pavement but to the systems and structures and policies that dull our imaginations for a world that truly has hope and good news and beauty for everyone. Parts of it will be hard. We who have been willfully blind will have to commit to noticing it all—the good and the bad, the ugly and the absent, the decay and despair. We will have to pay attention to inequality. We will lament. And we will learn to live as exiles from those who have walked the path before us. What we notice will leave a mark on us; we will be changed and converted. We will feel the responsibility to do something in return. It will feel like a blessing and a curse all at the exact same time.

PART ONE

AFFLUENCE

I firmly believe that our salvation depends on the poor.

DOROTHY DAY

1 ✶ THE WALLS OF ROME

I was teaching an English class in a high-rise apartment complex full of low-income families in Minneapolis—mostly immigrant and refugees from East Africa. The tenants' association paid for me to come and teach English, primarily to women who had never had access or exposure to education. It was a dream job for me, chaotic and joyful and never, ever boring. The women straggled into my class and settled heavily in their chairs, the first time perhaps in hours they had a moment to themselves. Papers and pencils were scattered on the tables in front of us. I taught them about the ABCs, how to hold pencils, how to have our eyes rove from the top left of the paper all the way down. We talked about our families, about grocery shopping, about rent problems, life in Africa versus life in America. We took a break in the midst of our three-hour classes for me to make them coffee and chai, pouring too much creamer and sugar into the mix, shooing away the cockroaches that always gathered in our makeshift kitchen.

I was trained to be a teacher, to be at the front of the room and command attention. To be an expert, to be listened to. But quickly I realized this wasn't what I wanted to be or what my students needed. We would interrupt an English lesson to talk about the actual problems they were facing—an eviction notice, a son getting in trouble at school, someone having a terrible headache, someone needing help reading a blood-pressure medication bottle. And I loved this because what I really wanted was to be of use, to be helpful. To make the lives of these incredible and complex women just the tiniest bit easier.

My classroom was loud, full of laughter, chairs scraping, women commiserating in languages that were decidedly not the one we were supposed to be studying. And none of it bothered me, except one thing:

the phones. Every woman had a small, compact, black cellphone—not a smartphone, just a utilitarian way for people to be reached in the case of emergency or missed appointments or reminders to pay bills. These tiny back phones never stopped going off, especially on Fridays. One such day I reached my limit. "Turn the phones *off*," I said, loudly. "*Off*." My students looked at me in surprise. They were quiet, for once, in the face of me trying to wield my influence, trying to muster up what little authority I was supposed to have. Finally, one of the women held up her little rectangle, the screen glowing green. "Teacher," she told me, "teacher, we cannot read, we never know who is calling."

The women around her nodded their heads. I stood up front, abashed at my ignorance. As their teacher I should know that to most of them, the numbers blurred together into the same indecipherable squiggles that covered the rest of our worksheets. They had to take every call because they had no way of knowing who was on the other line. It could be a family member in the camps in Kenya telling them they have no food and need money. Friday is payday, which is why the phones ring on this day. To ignore those needs would be a travesty, it would be unthinkable.

I went home that day and looked at my own phone. It did not light up on Fridays full of stories of people with no food in their bellies, of babies who were sick and the mothers who needed formula, of an illness that wiped out a caregiver. Living and working in refugee populations for the past decade had led me to feel secure in my belief that I was close to poverty, that I was starting to understand a bit how it worked in the world. But now I knew better: I always had been, and always would be, cushioned by the affluence of my life, by the community I was born into. I didn't know what it was like to be born hungry. And I didn't know how to be in a long-term relationship with those in the world who never, ever got their fill.

★ ★ ★

Affluence has shaped my life and therefore my imagination. I see this in my work with refugees, how it started with me believing myself to have something to offer to the poor and needy because I was born with more. It was a framework of charity, not righteousness—which in Hebrew can be translated as "justice." I wanted to help individuals out of my personal cache of goodwill and resources, but I was unprepared to engage in the systems and policies that led to such deep brokenness and inequality. Quickly I realized that my charity was a failure. I could not fix generations of trauma, war, economic oppression, and political persecution with a few English worksheets or a bag of donated clothes. Instead, I would need learn how to show up, sit down, and listen as best as I could, thinking about my role as a follower of God in a world that produced such vastly unequal opportunities for flourishing.

Later in life, I was surprised to find that the circumstances that felt to me like a crumbling of my worldview were actually moving me toward a more biblical one. One of my favorite Old Testament theologians is Walter Brueggemann, who reads the Hebrew Scriptures with an eye toward economics. In the stories, songs, and legal documents of Scripture he sees the common narrative is one of "the sustained struggle between the insatiable acquisitiveness of Pharaoh and 'neighborliness' in commitment to sharing the common good."[1]

The Israelites are marked as a new and chosen people not just by the one true God they worship but by how they approach wealth, economics, and the flourishing of the entire community in opposition to the greed of the powers all around. The God of the Old Testament is radical in that he didn't create humanity only to serve him—but this God of the Israelites cares about the very least in the community flourishing. This God cares about the land and wealth and how we use it to either exploit or to help one another.

In the New Testament this duality between the ways of pharaohs and the ways of Yahweh is expressed as the contrast between the kingdom of God and the kingdoms and powers of the world. Or, even more to the point, by Jesus simply telling his followers "you cannot serve both God and mammon" (the deity of money). God cares about how we operate our lives—including how we make, spend, and approach wealth—because God cares about people. God is well aware that people need food, shelter, and safety to live, as well as a society modeled on the radical concept of hospitality, to ensure that everyone can flourish.

This is why the continual comparison and contrast between the ways of a God of neighborliness and the ways of the Pharaoh/empire are important in Scripture. It is important for those of us who are embedded in the dominant culture of the United States to take the time to meditate on the ways of Pharaoh, who ruled off of predatory economic practices and was never satisfied. The Bible shows us example after example of empire and how it works in the world: places like Egypt, Assyria, Babylon, and Rome. It was striking for me to realize how many Americans seem to idolize these powerful entities. Walking around Washington, DC, is a testament to these desires: the white columns and monuments and buildings in were modeled after Roman architecture to let everyone know that the American experiment would have a similar ideology.

America as the new Rome: that is what the founding fathers envisioned. And, as John Dominic Crossan writes, we see similar threads between the two cultures. Roman imperial theology held that peace comes through victory—through military might and the affluence of the empire.[2] Many of the same arguments have been made for America's foreign policy and military intervention in recent decades and the ever-expanding desire to consume more and stimulate the economy. But Crossan and other theologians contrast the peace-through-victory approach of imperial powers with the work of Jesus. In Jesus we see peace coming through true justice for all and through the ultimate work of self-sacrifice.

Jesus is the lens through which we all must view our lives in the midst of empire. We cannot escape the political, social, economic, and religious realities around us, nor should we. But an ethic of neighborliness—how we put our love of God in action—should drive us to interrogate the pernicious values of empire that we find ourselves swimming in. The stakes are rather high, however. In the end Jesus was killed by an empire that found him threatening to the status quo. His body was nailed to a tree, left next to the side of a road to be a visible, decaying symbol of what happens when you subvert the powers of the world, when you insist that God's love goes beyond the borders we love to construct for ourselves, when you make it clear you will no longer serve the Pharaoh or his dehumanizing ways.

★ ★ ★

In the Bible wealth is a blessing from God—but it is one that can make us forget our neighbors, especially the most vulnerable. It is a blessing and a curse; both of these things are true, and because of this dual reality economics is a core preoccupation of the biblical tradition. Old Testament laws were very much concerned with how the people of God would live together in covenant community: it was assumed you would be close to those who were poor, and therefore you would be more likely to be invested in their future. Radical, some would say foolish, economic practices were put forth by God, including the Jubilee laws, where every fifty years the land would be returned to the original owners, slaves would be set free, and the earth would rest and lie fallow for a year. It should not be surprising that these laws were never fully followed, but Jubilee remains a sign to the rest of the world that God's ideal economy is one where righteousness shall flourish, which involves limiting the disparity between the wealthy and the poor, where creation is valued. God's ideal economy banks on the idea that you shall know your neighbor who is suffering and that you shall be compelled to do something about it.

Pharaohs are always looking to create the illusion that all is well—building pyramids or coliseums or white houses as shining monuments to earthly success. But these illusions are shattered the moment we understand how those monuments came to be: built on the unseen labor and heartbreak of the marginalized. This is why relationship is at the core of God's way of working in the world, and I see these values most commonly personified not in affluent communities but the opposite. People like my students intimately know both the blessings and the hardships of being connected to suffering and inequality at all times. There are those living in the shadows of the strip malls and city halls whose cell phones are always ringing, where a friend or family member is always in crisis, where generosity is always expected and nearly always given, sometimes at great personal cost. And there are other people, like myself, who have to wonder at the deafening silence in our own lives, our lack of connection to need and inequality that plagues our world.

Becoming a do-gooder, a teacher, a volunteer: these are the ways I tried to reach out because it was what I knew to do. Charity can sometimes feel like neighbor love, especially to the one giving it. But all too often it fails to address the roots of poverty. It baptizes the inequality of the world as normal—where some people give charity and others receive it, and it will always be so. The trouble with this narrative, born of affluence, is that we don't see these disparities, this hierarchy we have created, until it is much too late. Until we have effectively ruined any chance at a real relationship with God or with our neighbor. "Turn the phones off," I said that day in class, confident I was doing the right thing, unaware of my own ignorance of structures and systems of suffering. And my students, my friends, gently illuminated my world.

My own story is reflected in the pages of the Bible: how God uses the reality of the marginalized neighbor to check our natural desire to benefit from a predatory economy, of continuing on in a quest for more and more success and wealth and power. Neighbors change us if we let them. They reveal to me the walls I have built up in my own heart to not be responsible for my brothers and sisters in need. They point to the physical walls and the legal policies my country has designed to keep affluence in and poverty and need out. They show just how flimsy my theology is, how much I want to believe that everyone gets what they earn, that God really does operate like a cosmic vending machine in the sky. But walls, both psychological and physical, cannot stop the work of the Spirit of God. Even in the midst of policies and programs and closed borders, God sends neighbors to us, phones ringing wildly, hands patting our back, giving kisses on both cheeks. And until we learn to love these neighbors as God does, the promise of Jubilee, of an economy based in righteousness and not greed, will hang over our heads like a curse instead of the blessing that it is.

2 ✶ WHO IS MY NEIGHBOR?

I HAD A FRIEND WHO LIVED and worked with refugee communities. One day a woman reached out to her, asking, "Do you have any refugees I could come hug?" This woman was agitated, anguished even, about the political situation that kept pushing refugees to the top of the headlines. She was a good-hearted person, no doubt, but my friend was at a loss for words. Her neighborhood wasn't a zoo full of people that this woman could drop into and observe or hug somebody whenever she felt sad. But this woman, like so many, reached out to my friend precisely because of her lack of connection. She was trying to span the bridges our society had created, albeit on her own terms. And those terms dictated that some people were nameless, faceless groups of the miserable, always up for a nice woman to come in and comfort them.

I too have experienced many such offers of "help" and have polished my ministry of gently deflating these do-gooder dreams. The people in my neighborhood who have experienced forced migration don't need a hug from a strange woman. What they need are good neighbors. They need people to live next door to them, to send their kids to school with theirs, to vote for policies that protect instead of harm them. They need people whose lives are intricately bound up with their flourishing.

It's a hard message to give in my city—which, like so many in our world, is segregated by race and class. Asking people to do good, to give, to be charitable, becomes easy in these kinds of societies; asking them to be neighbors with those they most wish to help is not, since it points out an inconvenient truth that most of us try hard to forget all the time: some of us have worked hard to make sure we are only neighbors with certain kinds of people, and now we have to live with the results.

★ ★ ★

There is a famous parable Jesus told about a good Samaritan in Luke 10. It is about how a priest and a Levite—the pristine, untouched, religious, the followers of God—ignored a man who had been beaten by robbers and left for dead on the side of the road that went from Jerusalem to Jericho. It is a Samaritan man—someone Jesus' audience had been conditioned to despise from birth—who took care of the victim and found him shelter and clothes. There are many reasons people love and fear this parable. Jesus was telling the crowd that it is often the people we least expect who are the ones who actually do the work of God in the world, saving those who have been battered by our culture. He was telling us that the people who think of themselves as good often turn out to be terrible neighbors.

But I often think, too, about the man who asked the question that sparked the parable. We are told that a lawyer—an expert in the Old Testament law—wanted to test Jesus (Luke 10). So he asked the mother of all questions, "What shall I do to inherit eternal life?" Jesus turned the test back on him, shrewdly asking him to sum up the law—which the man had studied his whole life. "How do you read it?" Jesus asks him, all innocent. The man is a good student, he immediately sums up the entire work of Scripture: "You shall love the Lord your God with all your heart and with all your soul and with all of your strength and with all of your mind, and your neighbor as yourself." And Jesus replies, "You have answered correctly; do this, and you shall live."

But the lawyer is not satisfied with Jesus' answer. The lawyer could say all the words of what it meant to be good, to possess the keys to God's approval and favor and eternal life; but he did not understand them. We know this because in verse 29 it tells us he reached out to Jesus again, not done with the conversation. "But he, desiring to justify himself, said to Jesus, 'And who is my neighbor?'"

This verse haunts me more than any other in Scripture, for it defines the ethics of our time. How many of us have orchestrated our lives around this same question, buoyed by a life of continual self-rationalization? In truth, I don't really want the answer to that question *who is my neighbor?* I want to remain safe and secure, confident that I have accrued eternal life for myself, that I am a good person. But Jesus tells the lawyer, and he tells me and he tells you, that the good neighbor is the one who shows mercy to those who have been robbed and left by the wayside of society.

The irony is, the more you try to be the good neighbor, the good Samaritan with eyes to see the world, the more the battered and bruised bodies start to pile up. As one of my mentors once told me, you can only help so many people on the side of the road before you start to wonder where all of these damn robbers are coming from. The more you see a world that creates Jericho highways and profits off of there being a society full of both robbers and victims. The more you notice the outwardly righteous who either cannot or will not see their responsibility to alleviate the suffering, the more we might have to ask ourselves where we fit in the parable. I think about that priest and that Levite in the story, how they were so sure they were doing what was right. The Samaritan man possessed something they did not, something I am now on a perpetual quest for: curiosity at the way the world works and what our responsibility might be to each other.

★ ★ ★

The people who most hate talking about money are the rich. This is one reason I've come to appreciate the work of Rachel Sherman, a sociologist who studied the very wealthy in New York City.[1] She describes the lack of research on the wealthy—study after study talks about how poverty influences people but not affluence. One of the reasons for this is that wealthy people abhor talking about money. It is incredibly difficult to do research on this topic. But Sherman found more than fifty wealthy couples in New York City, the most unequal city in the world, to research, and the results are fascinating.

Several of the most important takeaways from Sherman's research are that wealthy people love to downplay their own privilege. This happened almost exclusively with people Sherman describes as "upwardly oriented." Their $1.5 million beach house is the smallest on the block; they struggle to keep up with the other families at their children's expensive private school. Someone always has a better penthouse. Nearly everyone, Sherman found, had a hard time articulating the reality that they were some of the richest people in the world.

Sherman also found that many of the wealthy people she talked to downplayed their wealth as a way of dealing with being on the top of an unequal system—one where the top 1 percent has more than the rest combined. But another way they coped is by believing that inequality and unjust social systems always had and always would exist. Therefore, they reasoned, they should strive to be good people and use their money wisely, rather than trying to change the system. In interviews many people brought up how they had earned their money. People who had inherited their wealth struggled the most with guilt; those who accrued wealth through their jobs as lawyers or bankers had no problem saying they had earned their money by working hard and thus had a moral right to it.

Talking about affluence and privilege is hard, but it doesn't have to be. I am continually grateful for the perspectives of people outside my own fold. Like Dr. Martin Luther King, for instance, who turned the discussion of consumerism and affluence upside down. Dr. King didn't talk about guilt, instead he loved to talk about how before we even get to work in the morning we have already lived a globalized life—our coffee grown in Latin America, our soap made in France, our bread grown by farmers in the Midwest.

I think about Dr. King, his head and heart full of the troubles of his country in the 1960s, himself and his family under the constant threat of assassination due to his work trying to get America to provide equal rights to all citizens, especially Black folk. And he took the time to consider the small aspects of his life—the coffee, the soap, the toast—

and asked us to do the same. This is the language he used—*behold*, *dependent*, *interconnected*. Right after talking about coffee and soap, Dr. King said, "All men are caught in an inescapable network of mutuality, tied in a single garment of destiny. Whatever affects one affects all indirectly. I can never be what I ought until you are what you ought to be."[2]

This is a beautiful reframing of the problem that runs on a loop in my mind. In the decades since King's life and death, our economy has only become more complicated. Phones made in factories in China, chocolate made by exploitative child labor in West Africa, clothing made in factories wherever it is cheapest. These are the kinds of things that overwhelm me when I start to pay attention. Consumerism—and a global economy that remains opaque in order to preserve the luxury of some and the suffering of others—feels deeply personal because it is. I am connected to real human beings through my purchases: my iPhone, my candy bar, my T-shirts. Am I responsible for their suffering in some way, or am I just a powerless cog in the machine? I am constantly battling numbness, one of the spiritual fruits of affluence. I become paralyzed by all the ways I can do wrong, all the neighbors I might have to care about if I truly start to view myself as responsible. Catholic theologian William T. Cavanaugh posits that the disembodied vice of greed is not so much what ails our society as it is an economic system based on detaching people both from production and consumption, leading to some pretty un-Christian modes of living. He says that no person really wants to impoverish a single mother in Latin America in order to buy cheap clothes—we are simply too detached from the process to be bothered by the unjust realities that we engage in.[3]

Dr. King pushed back against dehumanization and detachment in many forms. He looked at his own life and choices as a chance to live out a holistic ethic of a Christ-centered life: to practice neighbor love on the smallest levels and to build up the muscles of gratitude, dependency, and connection—all vital if we are to live and work for justice. Dr. King was inspired to look at his life, down to the items he used and where they were produced, by the parable of the rich fool and the barns in Luke 12. Jesus tells the story of a rich man who builds bigger and bigger barns in order to store all of his goods. The rich man tells his soul to eat, drink, and be merry. But God comes and tells him he is a fool instead, and that all his stored goods will end up going to someone else. Dr. King's interpretation of this story was that the rich man was a fool because he failed to realize he was dependent on others. And as a result, he was spiritually impoverished.[4]

As a privileged person in an unjust world, I see myself as a mirror image of the rich man building his barns or of the lawyer who asked Jesus, "Who is my neighbor?" There is a thinness to my idea of who my neighbor is that has dire consequences for my neighbors both near and far. I too have spent my days with my nose in the Good Book, searching for all the right answers, longing to present to God an airtight case of why I have been found perfect, why I am deserving of love. I am tired, however, of seeking to justify myself. Instead, I long for the eyes to see the bruised and battered of the world. I long to wake up with the curiosity it will take to one day make the world a highway safe enough for anyone to travel on.

3 ★ GETTING CURIOUS

For several years my husband and I lived in low-income apartments surrounded by neighbors from Bhutan and Somalia and Guatemala, by single mothers who grew up in generational poverty, by people who had experienced homelessness. A year or two ago I looked up where we lived on a map created nearly a century ago by the government for the express purpose of designating real estate value to various parcels of land. In the 1930s and 1940s the US government created the Home Owners Loan Corporation (HOLC) and sent out mortgage lenders, developers, and real estate appraisers to create maps of 250 cities that "color-coded credit worthiness and risk." The place where we lived was shaded in yellow, which categorized it as definitely declining: not a good investment. Across the street was a large red area: even more dangerous. The HOLC's reasoning for risk was thus: those areas contained the greatest Italian population in the city, and because there was a prevalence of "colored races" that constituted "a subversive racial influence." The reports, scanned and saved and uploaded to a website anyone can access today, go on to say that parts of this neighborhood would have been given a better classification if it weren't for the presence of so many immigrants and "colored people."[1] Alas, if only they hadn't lived there. My neighborhood would have been deemed valuable.

Curiosity made me look up this map, this website, tracing the lines of history that deemed some communities worth investing in while others were left to wilt in the absence of services and capital. What struck me was that this wasn't an accident. Nikole Hannah-Jones, a writer who works on segregation issues in education, once made the point that someone had hand-colored in those neighborhoods. Somebody, a real person just like me, had taken red and yellow markers and chosen to deem entire populations as hazardous to investors. Immigrants and Black Americans were left to struggle without bank loans or new businesses coming in, and they were strategically grouped together and then left without services afforded to White folks—a process we now call redlining, thanks to those simple pieces of paper that forged the fortunes of so many. Those maps caused some of my neighbors to live through decades of intentional disinvestment while my grandparents were busy cashing in on the American Dream of a house and a mortgage and their very own backyard. Looking at those color-coded maps was a transformative experience. It helped me—someone who grew up disconnected from both land and history—begin to see how something as small and tangible as a map and a marker can change the destinies and fortunes of generations. It was one small step on my journey of getting curious about how the world works and who it works for.

* * *

The Latin root of *curiosity* means "cure," which makes me wonder if it isn't a way to heal some of our oldest sicknesses. Like, perhaps, the "amnesia of affluence" that theologians point out in the Bible, and in our modern-day context. For myself, getting curious about the land, the actual space that I inhabit, has been the first step toward understanding where I am located in a vastly unequal economic world.

Besides the kingdom of God, the topic Jesus talked about the most was money. I think of those small, twisty, nearly inscrutable parables that Jesus told the crowds who followed him. Most of them were incredibly challenging to those who had ears to hear, especially if you had resources or thought that you had earned the right to hoard due to correct beliefs and actions. But there is an underlying sense of wonder to stories Jesus told, a sense of connection and yet also a deep unsettling of the rules we create to go through life.

Curiosity helps me pay attention to what I might otherwise want to miss: for some, the good news of the American Dream feels like bad news. I live in neighborhoods where I see the evidence of it everywhere: payday loan companies and fast food joints abound, but there are no green parks or community centers or apartments that are affordable to people working full time at minimum wage. Curiosity helps me flip the question upside down: What would good news for my lower-income neighbors feel like for me? Would it, just possibly, feel a bit like bad news to me in the beginning, if I wasn't used to a truly equitable world?

My home of Oregon remains one of the whitest states in the United States because that is how it was designed. At the beginning of their statehood, in the 1850s, Oregon outlawed slavery. But before anyone could congratulate Oregon for being so progressive, the state excluded free Black men from entering because they were worried these men would "intermix with Indians, instilling into their minds feelings of hostility toward the white race." In 1857 Oregon had the distinction of being the only free state admitted to the union with an exclusion clause—an exclusion clause in the Incorporated Bill of Rights, which prohibited Black persons from setting foot in the state without penalty of violence against their bodies.[2]

Although the laws were rarely enforced, the intentions worked, and the ramifications ripple onward. Currently, over 150 years after these laws were put into place, less than 2 percent of Oregon is Black. And from 1970 until 2017, the rates of homeownership for Black people in Portland plummeted by almost 40 percent.[3] Are we curious about why this is? Do we accept the unequal and unjust world we live in and then simply move on? Or do we follow the lead of Christians like Oscar Romero, a Jesuit priest in El Salvador, who wrote, "Not having land is a consequence of sin. . . . The land contains much of God, and therefore it groans when the unjust monopolize it and leave no space for others."[4] His faith led him to listen to those who did not have access to land, and his faith led him to see it as sinful that some monopolized what God so freely gave—and called it good.

Others, like Dr. King, went a step further. "Men convinced themselves that the system that was so economically profitable must be morally justifiable. . . . Their rationalizations clothe obvious wrongs in the beautiful garments of righteousness. This tragic attempt to give moral sanction to an economically profitable system gave birth to the doctrine of White supremacy."[5] Dr. King was talking about chattel slavery based on a hierarchy of race, which led to the boon of American production and wealth—for certain populations. It's the kind of economics that works so well that slave owners told themselves, much like the conquistadors, that they were doing God's work by evangelizing and Christianizing the African people they enslaved. As Jonathan Wilson-Hargrove so eloquently points out in his book, the vestiges of this "slave-holder" religion trickle down to all of us who were born into privileged groups.[6] And one of the ways White supremacy has so deeply enmeshed itself with both an economy that brutalizes and capitalizes on suffering is by getting those of us who have benefitted to not pay attention. White supremacy works by squashing curiosity that might center the voices whose backs have been broken by what others have called manifest destiny.

* * *

I have spent most of my life in the western half of the United States, but for three years my husband, small daughter, and I lived in the Midwest—in a gloriously chaotic and truly diverse city called Minneapolis. I spent those three years wandering around Somali malls and gawking at street signs in Hmong, rubbing shoulders with transplants from the South, being the minority for once in my life. When we came back to Portland after three very cold winters away, it seemed the city had changed overnight. The apartments we used to live in had long waiting lists. The surrounding rents were all out of our financial reach. The demographics had changed, or at least it seemed to us that way. We wandered on the leafy streets near our old complex, past all the shops that glittered with gentrification signposts—artisan backpack shops and soul food restaurants run by White people, hot yoga studios, and grocery stores where we couldn't afford to buy a piece of gorgeous, GMO-free fruit. Something in me ached at what was missing. The sameness, the homogeneity of the people walking and shopping and eating was shocking, especially after living in the vibrant and eclectic Midwest (something I would never have believed I would ever write until I had lived it myself).

After being away, after living in a city where people of difference actually had to learn to live and grapple with each other every day—Minnesota as a whole has around seventy-five thousand Somali-speaking immigrants, for instance, compared to the twelve thousand that Oregon has resettled—coming back to an increasingly gentrified Portland was like living in a washed-out photograph, the colors muted, both literally and figuratively. It felt like Portland had lied to us.[7]

Everywhere I looked, bumper stickers implored me to Keep Portland Weird. Slowly, I started to understand what people meant when they said this or put it on their car. They meant weird in a very precise and narrow and exclusionary way—the aesthetics of difference but with the insides all the same. The intentions of the individual people might have been good: they might truly believe they welcomed diversity or otherness or weirdness, but their systems had been built for another purpose. Like so many cities, schools in Portland were unequal and segregated. There were few affordable places where families in poverty could live. Rents kept rising and people kept leaving. Maybe people noticed this, or maybe they didn't. Maybe they felt sad and helpless and resigned. Or maybe they consoled themselves with those bumper stickers, with a few token examples of celebrating diversity while structuring their life in such a way that they didn't have to live in proximity to it.

Portland told me it was kind, that it loved difference, celebrated it, protected it. But Portland was mistaken. Like so many well-meaning White people, Portland is puzzled that its good intentions aren't enough in the face of strategic policies and practices designed to further inequality. And yet the myth of Portland that has captured the national imagination, the place where young and creative folks come to retire (thanks, *Portlandia*), continues blithely on, proud of its weirdness, even as it gets more and more consumable, generic, and homogenous. What Portland never told me, though, was that this was all very much on purpose. It had been planned long ago, back when the neighborhoods were colored red or yellow, when it first became best practice to discriminate and penalize Blackness and otherness.

When we moved back to Portland, the lack of sorrow for a city that was so homogenous, that was so truly unrepresentative of our world, shocked me. I looked at the faces walking by me, the beards and tight jeans and bicycles and expensive coffees. These are the things people normally fixate on when they want to talk about gentrification or mass displacement, when they want to talk about how things are changing. But I didn't care about those—they were just symptoms of a larger illness. Instead, I looked at the faces all around me and noticed how happy everyone looked. I noticed how no one seemed to mind that only a certain kind of person could afford to live there.

* * *

In the book *The Color of Wealth*, the authors state that "income can change on a dime, but wealth changes across generations." They go on to write that "an estimated 80 percent of assets come from transfers from prior generations."[8] Home ownership has historically been one of the most important ways to build wealth in the United States. And yet from 1930 to 1960 less than 1 percent of all mortgages were given to African Americans—precisely because of discriminatory housing practices like those red and yellow colored HOLC maps.[9] Being strategically cut out from one of the most concrete ways to accrue wealth has had historic consequences. And the reverse is also true: I myself am a product of people who were able to capitalize on a system that was built and designed for them.

Once I was at a workshop for people who wanted to use writing to change the world (oh, we were all so hopeful!). Our instructor invited a visiting lecturer, a woman who had grown up in generational poverty and trauma, and who wrote beautiful and sharp poems and prose about the dignity of people who are poor.[10] She went around the room and had us talk about our families—whether we grew up poor or not. Most of us hemmed and hawed, most of us tried to say that we were middle class or lower-middle class. None of us could say we were rich. I think I mentioned something about my family having an income that changed constantly—sometimes we were living in a nice suburban house, sometimes a converted trailer home, and once for a few months we lived out of an RV. But this woman, Julia, stopped the class. She pointed out how ashamed we were to talk about money. How most of us didn't grow up poor and were trying to explain that to her.

It was the first time I realized how much I resisted talking about money or my relative wealth. I realized I needed help in order to be honest about my place in the world and what God might be asking me to do with my privilege: my parents, who were White, had some college education and were able to offer some funds for my own education through their own assets—including home ownership. I grew up listening to conservative talk radio squawk about welfare mothers, but it was strangely silent on mortgage subsidies, federal scholarships, tax breaks for businesses and corporations, and sweet deals for developers looking to attract a certain type of neighbors.

The deep and dark tragedy of affluence is how it takes away curiosity, how it accepts the world as it is, how it conforms to the talking points of empire and Pharaohs. It keeps us from wondering why people of color tend to live in concentrated urban areas with a lack of services, why White folks flock to the suburbs on the backs of subsidies (and then back to the cities when it later becomes profitable), or why our cities remain segregated by class and race. Affluence hears all of these statistics and then looks around at its own neighborhood. Everything seems to be going okay; everything seems to be working out for them. It must have been all that hard work; it must have been deserved. To be curious about any other answer is to open wide the door of responsibility, of kinship, of strings that connect our well-being to the well-being of everyone else.

Those HOLC maps changed the way I viewed my city. It made me wonder every time I saw a bumper sticker. What do we mean when we say Keep Portland Weird? Do we mean to keep it redlined? Do we mean keep excluding immigrants and people of color and in particular African Americans from gaining access to property and wealth acquisition? Do we mean that we want to clutch tightly at our myths of pioneers like Lewis and Clark, who "discovered" a place already filled with people and an indigenous culture? I hope it is clear by now I don't have all the answers to these questions, that I am only just now starting to pay attention enough to start asking them, a thread that continues to unravel my carefully cultivated beliefs about how my world and country works. Perhaps this is why so many of us resist the discipline of getting curious. Perhaps we are rightly worried that the troubling revelations might never end.

4 ★ LOW, LOW PRICES

I was in Walmart looking for something, like everyone else. I wandered the aisles, keeping one eye on my loud and demanding child sitting in the cart, the other on the aisles around me, watching for a deal that would make my life simpler and easier and more affordable. I went down the row filled with detergents. So many choices. I didn't have a preferred brand, but I was drawn to the bottles and boxes that looked higher-end like they were nontoxic, natural, organic. Like they would actually be bringing forth goodness into my life, that my children would smell fresh and clean and chemical-free as they wandered through the earth. The sprigs of lavender pictured on these types of bottles, the sense that I was making the "correct" purchase in a world full of lurking evils and carcinogens—this all flashed through my mind in a few seconds. The mental load of consumerism is a hell of a burden, one we all take on willingly.

I looked at the prices and decided that I didn't need to buy anything today. I still had half a jug of detergent at home, and we could wait just a bit longer. At the end of the aisle, as I turned to head off toward another section, I saw a screen. It was a monitor showing me and my cart and my child as we wandered through the aisle. Filming in Progress, said the monitor. Shoplifters Will Be Prosecuted.

I looked around and then back at the little image of myself on the screen. It was as if I were a little god, watching those made in my own image prowl the aisles of Walmart. What else could such a god see? In an instant, I knew: God could see all the people, day after day after day, who didn't have enough money for soap and who took it quietly when they thought no one was watching.

★ ★ ★

"The God Who Sees" is one of my favorite descriptors in the Old Testament. It is, in fact, the first time in the Bible that a human gives God a name—and not just any human but a woman who had been used and abused, enslaved, and now an outcast—a woman who went on to become the mother of Ishmael, the patriarch of Islam.

Hagar was fleeing to the desert because she had been so abused by Sarah and Abraham, the supposed heroes of the faith. Alone, vulnerable, pregnant, she has no way to survive on her own. She is going to die. And then the angel of the Lord comes to her. He tells her that she will go back, she will have a son, and that her offspring will be multitudes. The angel says that the Lord has listened to her afflictions. Hagar then names the Lord El Roi, the God who sees. "Truly here I have seen him who looks after me" (Genesis 16:13). For her, the Lord is the opposite of everyone who has abandoned her, who wishes she would just vanish into thin air, that the wilderness would swallow up both her and her son.

The God who sees. This first name bestowed on God means something, especially for the forgotten of the world. Especially those who have suffered at the hands of patriarchy, misogyny, violence, selfishness, economic exploitation.[1] To know that you are not alone, to know that you are seen—sometimes this is all that is needed for the strength to keep carrying on. Even, especially, if you find yourself living in a wilderness, surrounded by people of plenty who would rather you didn't exist.

* * *

In Exodus 16 there was an old story of people needing something and God providing. Of the people of Israel wandering in the wilderness and of God sending them manna from heaven. Manna—as a child I imagined that it looked like tasteless Communion wafers, dissolving easily on the tongue. Manna, this sign of how God worked in the world, this food that came out of nothing, undeserving, to everyone. In the churches I grew up in, the story of God providing people with manna in the wilderness was told a bit as if it was a tragedy. The people sinned and then had to live in a wilderness—a refugee camp of their own making—and had to eat the same food every day for forty years. It was a punishment, a test from a God who wanted to prove something, to force obedience.

The Mennonites taught me to see different nuances in the text, how it shows a God who gives the chosen people decades of practicing what it looks like to value equality, to live in true righteousness/justice. Manna, bread given new every morning, was sent with strict instructions: no hoarding was allowed, no one was allowed to stockpile, to sell, to incur debts against their neighbors. If people tried to set up a black-market manna system, they awoke to see their stockpiles stinking and melted, covered with maggots. Those years in the wilderness with that sweet, ethereal bread was a forty-year relearning process, a reset on what the world is supposed to look like, how societies are supposed to be ordered. How to live together equally, no one taking more than their fair share.

Melissa Florer-Bixler, a Mennonite pastor, told me, "One of my favorite stories from the Talmud comes from a wondering by the rabbis—why did the manna come once a day instead of once a year? They tell a parable about a king and his son. When the king provided his son sustenance once a year, the son returned only once a year to thank his father. But when the son was given a small, daily provision each day, the child returned daily to thank his father. Daily thanksgiving, daily provision, daily a chance to receive love from a God who provides."[2]

But long ago that type of manna stopped falling from the sky, and it stopped being seen as miraculous by those who wanted more than a day's worth of food, by those who wanted to be able to hoard it without feeling guilty about it. Florer-Bixler says, "for one unique moment in God's history among people food was pure gift, a pure act of love. And as it was then, and as it shall be while people are on the earth, this arrangement became a place of discontent and faithlessness." The Israelites grumbled, they wanted variety, they were tired of the grace given every day, they wanted more control over their own destiny.

And this is the kind of culture I was born into, these were the values I absorbed with every meal, every trip to the grocery store, every time I rummaged around our well-stocked pantry. Affluence, even when it meant having more than others, became a virtue. It became a way of life, something to pursue: it became godly.

God understands the pull toward Pharaoh and his predatory economy, the backbone of which is the privileged hoarding resources. This is why the Scriptures give us the metaphor of manna, the threads connecting us all the way to Jesus and his body freely given to us. But how do those of us who were not raised on the ways of manna, of asking God for daily bread and being blessed by the miraculous ways that prayer is answered, learn to untangle our desires? In the Scriptures the ultimate check on the relentless desire for more is the reality of our neighbor. Especially the vulnerable ones, the widows, the orphans, the foreigners: those who benefit the least in a society orchestrated around power and hierarchy and patriarchy and ethnic and religious supremacy.[3] Living and being in community with vulnerable neighbors will change us. And, as always, the opposite is true. The farther we are away from those in need, either geographically or through power differentials, the more we can judge them and congratulate ourselves on our wisdom and prudence.

I think about this as I walk around Walmart, while I notice the boxes of Little Debbie Snack Cakes displayed prominently on end caps, the prices surrounded by smiling yellow logos (Low, Low Prices—I change it in my mind to Low, Low Wages).[4] I notice the woman who maybe forgot to pay for something being questioned by a checker, their voices rising. I notice the man speaking sharply to his son, who's asking for some candy. I notice the knives and guns and spray paint and toys being sold, all very close together. The last thing I notice is the security camera on the laundry aisle, and suddenly every family around me becomes a walking beacon of stories unknown, of a world where clean clothes are a privilege and a luxury that we do not afford to everyone. I know how affluence works, how different it is from a God who provides manna, who gives enough for everyone as long as some people don't hoard. How affluence needs segregation and amnesia to thrive, how it convinces us to forget God and instead take pride in our own choices and abilities. I know how affluence works because I see it in myself. I am forever trying very hard not to notice a world as unkind as the one I actually live in.

* * *

God does not dream of a world where banks foreclose on up to ten thousand homes a day (as happens in some communities in the United States). God is not pleased that half of all American children will live in a house at some point that uses food stamps to survive or that two-thirds of all minimum-wage workers are women. God doesn't accept as normal the truth that in 2013 four out of five Americans lived in danger of falling into joblessness and poverty while nearly half of Americans were considered poor or to have a low income.[5] This is not how God wants the world to work. These are the statistics that keep God up at night, ever watchful of the vulnerable. Are we keeping watch with God? Or do we prefer to slumber on?

Just as poverty is on the rise in the United States, so too is a world in which luxury is continually venerated and normalized, even as it is reserved for fewer and fewer people. The United States is more unequal than at any time since 1928, right before the Great Depression. We are edging back toward a world where a small concentration of people contain vast amounts of power, influence, and wealth. The richest 1 percent of Americans own more wealth than the bottom 90 percent combined.[6] It is far less likely that a poor American will rise from poverty to riches than a poor Canadian, German, or French person.[7] Even China has now surpassed the United States in terms of sheer numbers of people rising out of poverty in their lifetime.

In 2008 the CEO of Walmart made as much in one hour as many of his full-time employees made in a year. Are some people really worth that much more than others? We would most likely say no, but our economy says otherwise. We talk about the immorality of the poor but never the wealthy, and this is very much on purpose. While these statistics are sobering, so too is the response many of us have to them—the shrug of the shoulders, accepting the extreme inequality as a by-product of the supposedly free market. We accept inequality, and we even add to it. We penalize shoplifters, but never the businesses owners making thirty times as much as their employees. We only have eyes for certain kinds of wrongdoing, it would seem. And in the end it props up the world to continue to reward those at the very top while making life ever harder for those struggling to survive.

★ ★ ★

I went home from Walmart and did a quick Google search: what are the most commonly shoplifted items in the United States? Each item contained a Hemingwayesque short story within itself: pregnancy tests, diabetic test strips, baby formula, cigarettes, energy drinks, pain medication. These real-life necessities were interspersed with more unsurprising items like cell phones and televisions—items that can easily be resold for profit. Cheese and raw meat are two of the most common food items stolen, and the Bible has the distinction of being the most stolen book in the world. Part of me can't help but think that God is pleased with this—all of those Scriptures passing like contraband to those who most need them.

These lists are interesting, heartbreaking, and infuriating all at the same time. They were also news to me, as was the Filming in Progress notification in Walmart. It was a sign pointing to inequality, that my reality is different from those of so many of my neighbors. A clear, devastating sign that our society is failing to love our neighbors experiencing poverty. But I almost missed it, almost lost myself in the dreams of buying up a better world—lavender-scented, chemical-free clothes for my own precious family.

William Cavanaugh believes that desire in a consumeristic society keeps us distracted from the desires of those who are truly hungry.[8] It numbs us not only by encouraging us to want more and more but also by negating our God-given desire to work toward the common good. Consumeristic societies, like the one I live in, only exist by making the individual supreme. Everywhere we look there are people who are seen by God in an empire that despises and devalues them, even as it exploits them for profit. Learning not just to see but to learn from them is the only cure I know for finding our way out of the never-ending maze of the American Dream.

These teachers—the Hagars—will continue to find ways to reach those of us who are privileged. They'll set up their tents under freeway overpasses, forcing us to remember that not everyone can find safe and affordable housing. They'll keep undertaking the dangerous journey into our country, working jobs that most people will not and accepting the risks of living in the shadow economy because it's better than the violence and poverty they came from. Or they'll the risk fines and the jail time, the possible prosecution, for taking a box of soap when they have no money. They will confront us in the places we least expect; they will burst the walls of consumerism and apathy we build up. They will force us to see, even if we don't want to. Because it is in their nature. They are made in the image of the One Who Sees, the one who will never turn his eyes away.

5 ★ HOW NOT TO BE A MILLIONAIRE

I LISTENED TO A POPULAR CHRISTIAN FINANCIAL PODCAST the other day. The man who runs the program is famous to many Christians. In many ways I agree with him and appreciate the work he has done. His tireless rants against debt soothe my little activist soul, and the frugal person in me rejoices at the constant talk of learning to simplify, to refuse to give in to consumeristic or materialistic impulses. But when I look at them in the larger context of American society—a capitalistic society that is increasingly becoming more and more unequal, with more and more people falling into poverty—the popular messages spread far and wide to the faithful Christians disturb me more and more.

The episode I listened to the other day was about how anyone can become a millionaire (this wasn't an outlier either—this company regularly hosts conferences and events revolving around the idea of "everyday millionaires"). This guru espouses a basic approach over and over again: work hard, pay off your debts starting with the smallest to the largest, live within your means, and then enjoy the fruit of your labors. (And don't forget to be generous!)

This program works for many people, which is why it's so successful. People need encouragement and incentive to learn how to budget, how to tell wants from needs, to make clear connections between what they earn and what they spend. The program is part advice column, part celebrating those people who have done it, who have achieved the American Dream of being debt free, of paying off their mortgage, of being a millionaire.

The only problem is, being financially safe and secure isn't a major theme of Scripture—but unjust economic practices are. I want to see predatory lending end as much as anybody, and I long to see my neighbors and myself freed from consumerism. But I need and want a bigger dream than the idea of becoming a millionaire. I need a dream that encompasses God's dream for the world: that everyone would flourish, that everyone would have what they need to thrive as the image bearers they are.

★ ★ ★

My husband and I convened a group of people from our church to talk about money: our money, their money, and what we were supposed to do about it in the light of global and local poverty. We used a curriculum called Lazarus at the Gate, which was put together by several scholars, theologians, and Christian ethicists.[1] It was deliciously awkward and felt slightly transgressive to be so upfront about money in a community. We asked each other to write out a household budget and share it, and be held accountable for living a life of more generosity.

The more we met and talked about money, the easier it got. It became normalized to bring to light the discomfort we often felt in the corners of our minds as we navigated how we made and spent our money. At the end of the curriculum we pooled some of our money together and brainstormed people and places to give it to. The Lazarus at the Gate curriculum centers on the biblical concepts of living gratefully, justly, simply, and generously. It was the first concept that was most difficult for me: one of the suggested ways to practice gratitude was to say a prayer of thanksgiving every time you paid for groceries or any other purchase. I felt supremely silly at Safeway muttering, "Thank you, God, for your provision," as I swiped my credit card. But I did that every day for a week, and it broke loose something in me that was trying desperately to keep my money and how I spent it separate from how I related to God.

We talked about shame and discomfort, and we dreamed up ways we could live more simply and in a spirit of reciprocity to both creation and our vulnerable neighbors. We conspired together ways to be able to bless other people, to take joy and delight in what we had been given. Slowly I felt both my heart and my fingers opening up; I realized how necessary and vital it is to be in a community of people who can remind us of our call to care for each other, to listen for the voice of the Spirit of God who surprises us continually with ways to bless others if we only have the courage to ask.

* * *

Some days I dream about starting my own radio show about money. Instead of highlighting all the success stories of families who have eaten beans and rice for five years in order to pay off their mortgage, I would only take calls from people who had tried very hard to follow the six easy steps to be a millionaire and who were thwarted by both systems and policies that punish large portions of our society: people who have experienced job losses or who have prison records or crippling health bills or have family members who desperately need financial help; people who experience racism and sexism and xenophobia, who don't have equal access to opportunity. I would let them come on my show and pour out their stories of heartbreak, of failure, of not making it. I am almost positive nobody would want to listen, but I wish they would. Because when well-meaning, well-intentioned privileged people hear only the financial success stories, they are being discipled in how to judge and belittle all of those who fail in the landscape of the American Dream.

When I was growing up I always strove to "live within my means." This is sound financial advice for the middle class, especially for those prone to self-righteousness like myself. I have always been frugal with money and have worked at least part-time since I was a junior in high school. I scrimped and saved to pay my college tuition and to take out as little debt as possible. I did not attend prestigious or fancy schools. I ate ramen and peanut butter-and-jelly sandwiches and little else for years. I did all of this, and I felt extra virtuous. I felt spiritual, even. I felt secure in knowing I was doing what was right with my money, and as a result I felt free to judge all of those who I felt were doing it wrong, who I felt were spending beyond their means. And it quickly veered from silently judging my peers who bought expensive cocktails at restaurants or drank $5 cappuccinos to questioning why a lower-income family would own a flat screen TV.

The problem with easy dominant culture mantras like "live within your means" is that they give the privileged more ammunition to judge those who aren't making it while at the same time it makes no moral demands on those who make more than enough. If living within your means becomes one of your mantras, then who's to say it's wrong to buy a second or third beach home if you can afford it? It gives those with wealth permission to spend without constraint.

Eventually, something changed in me: I started to hear the non-success stories and let them sink in. I didn't realize how much I had changed until a member of my husband's family, who worked at a grocery store, told me once how disgusted they were to find a woman buying dozens of packages of hot dogs and buns with her food stamps. "Can you imagine?" this person said incredulously. "Using her food stamps to buy food for a party?" I could, actually, imagine this scenario. I myself had been fed by people who used what little they had to invite others into celebration. I knew many different people who do not make a living wage in the United States and who supplemented their income with food stamps. These friends used what they had been given to bless others. I saw the generosity in this gesture while others only saw excess. We've been trained to be angry at the "excess" of using government aid to feed people, instead of working to end a system that pays people poverty wages. I wonder why that is?

One of my heroes is Dorothy Day, the founder of the Catholic Worker Movement. She, along with her cofounder, Peter Maurin, was obsessed with the idea of helping create a world where it was easier to do good. Dorothy was a convert to Catholicism in her thirties and saw a clear connection between the social teachings of the Catholic Church and social action. Day and Maurin started houses of hospitality where the desperate could come and eat and sleep and talk about the issues of the day. The early days of the Catholic Worker Movement were filled with homeless men crowding her apartment and the weekly newspaper she banged out on her typewriter and sold for a penny a copy that highlighted the stories of injustice and the work of the Church. It was chaotic, it was difficult, it was aspirational.

Dorothy was fond of telling people not to call her a saint, saying it made her actual thoughts and teachings too easily dismissed. She truly believed that we all had a responsibility to each other, especially the poor. She believed the works of mercy were the hallmarks of Christian discipleship: feed the hungry, water the thirsty, clothe the naked, shelter the homeless, visit the sick and the prisoner, and bury the dead. She had many reasons to despair at the way the world was going in the midst of the Great Depression—the thousands of men in line for bread, the abject poverty in the city, the corruption in the Church. But in her private journals she often took the time not to write about the great injustices but instead the simple pleasures that delighted her: a piece of pie and a cup of coffee. Rereading a favorite Dostoevsky novel. Listening to classical music in a chair by the fire. She declared these small moments were vital to her long-term work. She called them her duties of delight.[2]

Dorothy Day is a failure in the eyes of the world, including Christians who strive to be millionaires, who think the best way to change the world is to influence it on its own terms. I think about her, how she was able to live in true solidarity with the poor and the sick and the sad for so many years. I also want to experience the duty of despair and the duty of delight. I want to live in the tension of the idea that God might want us to be a part of righting the wrongs in the world, that we might be called to give up what we have hoarded and learn how to be open and generous. It might be awkward. It might get uncomfortable. It might feel too small in light of the magnitude of the inequality of the world. But as Dorothy Day wrote, "We can throw our pebble in the pond and be confident that its ever widening circle will reach around the world. We repeat, there is nothing we can do but love, and, dear God, please enlarge our hearts to love each other, to love our neighbor, to love our enemy as our friend."[3]

Dorothy Day knew she would never be held up as financial success; her work was often either mocked or put on a pedestal, neither of which were comfortable spots. But she didn't care. "We confess to being fools and wish that we were more so," she wrote in an editorial for the *Catholic Worker* in 1946. "What we would like to do is change the world—make it a little simpler for people to feed, clothe and shelter themselves as God intended them to do."[4] If we should choose to live so foolishly like Jesus, we will be rewarded not so much with earthly pleasures but with the imagination like Dorothy had to hope another world could be possible. That we can live simply, justly, generously, and most of all gratefully: both for the blessings of our money and for the blessings of our neighbors who teach us how costly wealth can be to our souls.

6 ★ LAMENT FOR THE LAND

Certain parts of Portland historically have been redlined—places White people deemed unworthy and grew to see as hazardous. These districts are primarily in the north and northeast section and are where 75 percent of our city's African American population used to reside because it was the only place they could get a loan. Today, a person walking around these parts of Portland will see hundreds of "Black Lives Matter" signs. They are placed in front of gorgeous old Craftsman-style homes—homes that now, after decades of inequality, are finally deemed desirable. I see the signs everywhere, standing on their rickety metallic legs, proudly proclaiming their message of inclusivity.

But I hardly see any actual Black lives in that neighborhood. They have been pushed out to the surrounding suburbs by rising rents, scattered like seeds in the winds of capitalism, their institutions left behind to adapt or die, their roots spreading out in all directions, looking for a place to regroup.

I wonder how much those signs cost. A few dollars, perhaps. But the relief it must give the homeowners is incalculable.

★ ★ ★

Jeremiah 29:11 is a verse I often heard growing up: "'I know the plans I have for you,' declares the Lord, 'plans to prosper you and not to harm you, to give you a hope and a future'" (NIV). But it wasn't until after I was friends with refugees for many years that I began to see the extra layers of this verse. As a serious-minded Christian, and one who went to Bible college, I still had a hard time placing myself in the biblical narrative. I had what might be called the problem of familiarity—I was too close to many of the stories to see them clearly.

But one day, staying at a beach house owned by friends of my parents, staring at a picture of a lighthouse with the familiar words of Jeremiah written on it, something snapped. In a gorgeous setting, in someone's third house, it suddenly struck me how uncomfortable I was with out-of-context Scriptures. Especially if they turned the living Word of God into nothing more than a bland promise from a faceless deity that my life was destined for something good.

The book of Jeremiah was written to a devastated people, people who struggled mightily to reconcile their faith in a living God with the suffering they experienced as their world crumbled and they became the marginalized in a society built on power and wealth. Going back and reading Jeremiah 29 in context—the chapter is called "A Letter to the Exiles"—I found a poignant word of solidarity for the displaced: a fresh vision to build houses, settle down, make gardens, marry, have children, seek the peace and prosperity of the city that you were exiled to by God. To imagine a new future out of the ashes of the old.

It's a gorgeous promise in Scripture, but it isn't necessarily for me. As a third generation American, I'm not living in exile, nor am I in any danger of it. I have more in common with the Babylonians, the oppressors. The promise of flourishing is peripheral to me. But it still means something. It opens me up to asking why exile is such an important theme in the Bible. It opens me up to wondering if I could be living in Babylon. It opens me up to wondering how the idols of Babylon might have become my own.

★ ★ ★

Gentrification is a big deal in Portland. Gentrification is not fundamentally about hip coffee shops moving into poor neighborhoods or rising rents or even the forced displacement of people. Movement, and change and growth are not necessarily things to be feared, nor are they all bad. Integration—finding a way to live in places where there is a real diversity of incomes and backgrounds—has benefits for nearly everyone, from raising test scores in schools to encouraging the wealthy to give more.

Gentrification occurs when certain groups of people capitalize on the historic and strategic disinvestment of communities of color. As Peter Moskowitz writes in *How to Kill a City*, "It's not that most poor people or people of color hate the idea of anyone moving to the city, but that gentrification almost always takes place on top of someone else's loss."[1] Gentrification is the pursuit of affluence by people of privilege in a world where the scales have always been tipped. Gentrifiers are unified by their lack of curiosity to the ways the American Dream has been particularly good to them. Gentrification is waiting for the coffee shop that caters to your taste to open up before you spend money in the neighborhood. It's waiting until the local schools have a more acceptable diversity ratio before sending your kids there. It's capitalizing on what's best for you and yours while continuing to disinvest in those communities that have been erased from the narrative of the American Dream. It's putting up a sign that says certain lives matter, even as you profit off of their displacement.

* * *

Theologian Lisa Sharon Harper writes that "Shalom is what the kingdom of God smells like." She goes on to say that "if one's gospel falls mute when facing people who need the good news the most—the impoverished, the oppressed, the broken—then it's no good news at all."[2] For quite some time now I've been paying attention to who the good news of the American Dream is good for. Now it's time to be oriented in the other direction, to train my eyes and ears toward those who have been saying consistently that all is not well.

Jeremiah 29:11 was never intended to be an inspirational poster in someone's beach house, especially in an area where some own multiple homes while others cannot find a safe place to lay their heads. But it contains within it the seeds for what those of us who are closer to the power and status of the Babylonians are to do. Those of us from the dominant culture are invited to pay attention to the inequality in the systems that have benefited us, and we're invited to move our gaze elsewhere. To become downwardly oriented, obsessed with shalom not just for ourselves but for the people who are struggling the most in our midst. We are to help the exiles within our society to flourish: to plant gardens, find housing, nurture and grow their families. When we do this, we are promised that we too will finally find the peace that we crave. We will be rich in love, and in the joy of seeing God's dream for the world come alive before us.

★ ★ ★

In the apartments where we lived on the edge of Portland, the rent kept rising like a river about to overflow. Every year the monthly rents climbed over a hundred dollars a month. Our neighbors, mostly recently arrived refugees and immigrants, did not know how they could keep up. My husband had a good job and still it was a shock to us to get the bills, ever higher. Our apartments weren't getting any nicer (there were still bugs and mice and no screens on the windows) but we were paying more and more money.

We watched as the dumpsters behind the apartments filled with furniture, the tell-tale sign of evictions piling up. We watched as notices went up for new developments being built in the neighborhood, revitalization projects that boasted the promise of open-air markets, job share sites, and condos. I walked the neighborhood with my two children in tow, anguished at the thought of everyone I loved leaving because they couldn't pay the rent anymore. But what was I to do?

One day I went to a meeting about a new proposed site. They asked the community for their input, so I gave mine. I went up to the microphone in front of a long table filled with city council members. They looked at me, unblinking, and I shrunk inside myself. My voice wavering slightly, I told them what our neighborhood needed most was affordable rents, a green park for children to play in, and a community space that was free where we could have English classes or weddings or quinceañeras. The man who was in charge of the project gave me a tight smile.

"All of that sounds great," he said. "But we have to make sure there are income generating elements, or this project won't be viable."

I felt as small and as foolish as a child. There I was blathering on about parks and community centers to people who knew much more about the economy of my neighborhood than I did. I sat down. I knew nothing would be changed. And yet forever in the record of that meeting would be my tiny, quavering note of dissent. One neighbor, saying that green spaces, community spaces, places that were not necessarily profitable but were desired and necessary and deserving. My lament would be typed, filed, and ultimately ignored.

Now it is a few years later, and the rents continue to go up. Neighbors have left or are leaving. We work out our laments both by voicing our concerns and by organizing with others to advocate for renters rights, to protest developments, to plead with developers to think about the families that need affordable housing. I walk by the site of the place where the revitalization project is supposed to be coming. They fenced off the old park and it has sat unused for over two years. My children cling to the fence and ask me why we can't go in there anymore. I tell them something is going to be built, someday a new place for new neighbors is coming. But for now, it remains closed to us and to our community. The people who live here, the ones with children longing for a play structure or a green space to run around, walk by signs that proclaim that one day it will all be made new. By that time, I wonder how many of us will remain.

7 ✶ TRUE GENEROSITY

Rani did not make it to my son's birthday party. She had started working the night shift, so she had been sleeping. A few days later, at the English class I teach for parents in our community, Rani told me she had a present for my son. He was sitting next to me, like he sometimes does during class, his hair golden blond, swinging his legs off of the cafeteria bench. I saw her take the paper envelope, the kind you get at a bank, and put it into my toddler's chubby little hand. "Oh, Rani," I said, trying to appear happy and regretful. "No, no, no. He doesn't need the money." She nodded her head vigorously, smiling at me, and kept trying to get my baby to take it. Two-year-olds don't care about envelopes, but he smiled at her, his dimples flashing, and when I told him to say thank you to her, he did.

Sometimes Rani takes pictures of my blond baby and sends them to her family in Myanmar. She wants them to know she has American friends, that she is doing okay here—even though her husband just got laid off from his warehouse job because he hurt his back, even though she is only getting two days a week at her housekeeping job when she really needs five. At home, I opened up the envelope and took out a brand-new crisp $50 bill. I should have felt grateful, but instead I started to cry.

★ ★ ★

I am forever being given things by people who can be perceived as poor: food mostly but sometimes money, sometimes long, sad, or strange stories, sometimes hugs, and sometimes green tea with hints of cardamom or ginger. My children as well are constantly receiving gifts, to the point that they beg to go visiting in the apartments of our friends. They know they will be showered with love and affection, and they are right.

But the privileged part of me doesn't know what to do with these realities. I don't know how to be grateful in a world where I was taught that I was the one to give to those in need. But the people I think of as needy would bristle at such a description; they would be offended at the categories the world puts them in. Sometimes I wonder if they see it in my eyes, as hard as I try to hide it.

I often find myself paralyzed with shame, living in such close proximity to people who remind me constantly that my reality is not the same as theirs. My husband, a therapist and one of the kindest men the world has ever seen, tries to gently tell me that shame is never very helpful in the larger picture. Guilt, at least, can point out that something is wrong or indicate places where we have done or benefited from injustice; guilt can hold us accountable for our actions. But shame is a far murkier monster; indeed, I imagine it in the shape of a serpent. Shame is the whisper not that what you have done was wrong but that you, at your very core, are wrong. This is a lie and one that deserves to be crushed under the heel of a God who loves us.

Talking about affluence brings up shame for some people. So does paying attention to how unkind America is toward those without stable incomes or homes or families. So does asking people to interrogate their pasts, to think through the systemic factors that maybe benefited them and harmed others. But shame is unhelpful. I should know because I experience quite a bit of it. And no matter how much I wallow in shame, it doesn't actually make the world a better place for my neighbors. It doesn't undo how high the rents are, how backbreaking manual labor is, how the only shifts my friends can work and still take care of their kids are at night.

When my friend Rani gave my son that $50 bill, the shame bloomed in my chest until I sobbed. When my friends cook extravagant meals for me on limited budgets and in the midst of a busy life, I sometimes can barely eat I am so choked by the knowledge of my privilege. When my daughter excitedly wants to bring home a new umbrella from school, I turn and whisper that we don't need it, that we should save it for the other kids, and I see the confusion grow in her eyes, her cheeks becoming pink.

The older I get, and the more people my life crashes into, the more aware I am about how debilitated I am in my ability to receive. To receive the truth of our hard world, to receive gifts from those who in my eyes have so little, and to receive the message that even though I am not perfect, I am still loved.

* * *

One time Rani and I took the MAX train to attend a rally together. We had made signs and were going to protest the genocide that was happening in her home country. It was a solemn affair to be sure, but we were happy to be together, going downtown to add our voices to the chorus. A few stops in on the train, a man came walking by our seats, asking people for money. He was old and worn-looking, a baseball cap on his head. Nobody in our section looked at him. I smiled and shook my head: no, sorry, I don't have any money. Black purse in her lap, Rani opened it and got out her wallet. She snapped it open and I could see a $5 bill. She took it out and said, "Yes, here, for you." The man took it, surprised, and said, thank you. Then he looked at her, his eyes taking in her head scarf, and stammered out as if asking a question, "God, God bless you?" Rani simply smiled and nodded and turned back to me.

"If you give money," she whispered to me, "If you give money to people who need it, then when you are in trouble you will get money. Do you understand, Daniella?" I did understand. But still, that $5 was so hard-earned that it pained me to know that I could not control what that man in the baseball cap would do with it. In her own words Rani tried to tell me how there are different types of people in the world. There are people, like our mutual friend Hafsa, who, when they get a dollar, carefully place it in their purse and close it: saving it, watching it, taking care of it. "And then," Rani laughed, then there are people like her. "I get money," she told me, "and it flies out." She waves her hands outward. Clothes for her children, eating at restaurants, going to the Indian buffet, money, money, money, until it is finished. "Do you understand, Daniella?" I do understand, Rani, I do.

This is how my friend understands the world. She is generous because she has been in need. She has been wealthy and she has been very poor, and now she works hard to stay afloat in a land of rising rents and insurance and bills to pay. She does not go through life with a scarcity mentality as I do. She reveals my imagination to be one that has been trained in the ways of the pharaohs of old: there is never enough. We need to hoard, and we are justified in literally working people to death to accomplish our goals. If I was listening to the Spirit, I would have followed Rani's example and given that $50 bill she shoved into my hands away to any person who asked, believing that I had a role in providing for others just as I trusted that my own needs would be provided for. But I didn't because shame had stunted my imagination for generosity. I suppose I deposited that money in our bank. I don't remember because I try hard not to think about it.

* * *

For all the Bible has to say about wealth, it constantly praises the poor. In recent years, as I've read the Gospels with my neighbors in mind, I have been astonished by this. In the Gospel of Mark, for instance, nearly every encounter Jesus has depicts the marginalized as the faithful ones. The poor, the sick, the demon possessed, the outcasts, the hungry, the women. And conversely, it paints a powerful picture of those who were constantly arguing or trying to entrap Jesus, who were constantly missing out on the liberating presence and work that Jesus came to do. It was, of course, the good people. The religious ones. Jesus' own family. The ones who were considered successful, charitable citizens.

I wonder about this quite a bit because it relates directly to me. Why did the good news of Jesus feel so much like bad news to those who had affluence, autonomy, safety, and power? My husband and I argue about this sometimes. He doesn't believe Jesus ever used guilt or shame to motivate people, because that isn't how love works. Perhaps he is right. But still, when I read the Scriptures, I see story after story about how the educated, the rich, the religious, and the powerful not only missed out on Jesus' message but actively responded in ways that were angry, defensive, depressed, and eventually violent. Jesus, I believe, did not want people to live in cycles of guilt and shame and fear.

But Jesus was committed to telling the truth. And when we're forced to confront the truth of a world that has been kind to us but not to others, we can start to feel as though we are horribly bad, impossible to redeem, implicated without any hope of forgiveness. We can feel the spread of shame, and so most of us do what is perfectly natural. We stop thinking about it as soon as possible, in whatever way we can manage. We are terrified of having our greatest fear realized: of waking up to the reality that we are not good, we are not wanted, and we are not loved.

The antidote to affluence is not shame. It is, instead, thanksgiving. This is not a truth I learned on my own but one that has been revealed to me by my friends who excel in the duties of delight and gratitude and celebration, tempered by their very hard realities.

Indigenous scientist and writer Robin Wall Kimmerer visited a school on the Onondaga Reserve in New York, where every day the students recited the Thanksgiving Address—a very old and long and beautiful poem that starts their every school day. Very different from the quick mumbled grace a Protestant Christian might say at the dinner table, the Thanksgiving Address takes its time to thank various elements of the earth—water, wind, fire, plants, animals, and more. At the end of each section there is a time to invite the listener to agree, to come back to the mutual of understating: "We give thanks to the stars, who are spread across the sky like a jeweler. . . . With our minds gathered as one, we send greetings and thanks. . . . Now our minds are one."[1]

Kimmerer writes about the importance of those words: both the thanking of specific elements and the refrain "now our minds are one." She calls it a "statement of solidarity, a Bill of Responsibilities" that is couched in gratitude. Kimmerer sees in the Thanksgiving Address a radical discipline of cultivating a culture of gratitude that is vital to all life on earth. She believes true gratitude is couched in reciprocity where each person—human or not—is bound to each other in a reciprocal relationship. And this makes us unique among creation: "It is said that only humans have the capacity for gratitude. This is among our gifts."[2]

Learning to say thank you to my friends like Rani strengthens my faith in a God who bestows good gifts freely and infuses what could become a hierarchical relationship with mutuality. When I practice gratitude, it draws me into a reciprocal relationship with my neighbors, where I see their full humanity as distinct individuals with gifts to offer me. Learning to receive meals, clothes, affection, and even money from my friends and neighbors has renewed an ethic of thankfulness in me—even to the point where I am more likely to notice the seasons, the flowers, birds of the air, and the insects all working busily in tandem. Kimmerer sees the same connection: "Thanksgiving reminds us of how the world was meant to be in its original condition. . . . [W]hen we can no longer see the stars because of light pollution, the words of Thanksgiving should awaken us to our loss and spur us to our restorative action. Like the stars themselves, the words can guide us back home."[3]

Kimmerer was changed by listening to the voices of children chant the Thanksgiving Address: thank you to all the elements, let all our minds agree together in this gratitude. And she said she couldn't help but feel wealthy as she listened to the words. The Thanksgiving Address went on and on, so many reasons to be grateful, so many reasons to be present. So many entities to feel responsible to and for. What can sometimes feel like a burden to me just needs the lens of thanksgiving to set it right: what a richness of human experience God has gifted me. What a wealth of people, plants, and animals I have the privilege of being connected to.

★ ★ ★

There is a verse in the Bible that has always puzzled me. In the books of Luke and Matthew it says that Jesus had a reputation for being both a glutton and a drunkard. He was partying too much with tax collectors and sinners. In a world where many people lived in abject poverty—indeed, a large percentage of Jesus' community perhaps did not even know where their next meal was coming from—Jesus hung out with people who were wealthy enough to throw the kind of parties that earned him a reputation.

This does not fit with my mental image of Jesus. In my mind he usually appears sober and disappointed with the world, just like I am. But here we have it, in this bizarre book, that Jesus was a storytelling agitator who ate and drank his fill in a world full of suffering. I don't understand it, Jesus modeled how to live in a world where affluence and poverty coexist side by side, just like they do in my own city. I think Jesus understood the importance of both lament and celebration, and that there was a time for each.

Recently, my friend Ayana got my children Christmas presents. Ayana doesn't celebrate the holiday herself because she is Muslim. Her own children get very modest gifts for Eid—usually some new clothes and maybe a favorite meal. But she bought my kids gifts and presented them right in the plastic bags from the store. I squirmed in discomfort. My children did not need toys, and this was too much money coming from my friend who had four children and a husband who worked nights at the convenience store. I hadn't bought her children Eid presents; did this make me a terrible person? While these thoughts skittered through my brain, my children joyfully opened the plastic shopping bags. My daughter got a baby doll with a tiny pacifier, which she loved. My son pulled out a cartoonish gray object shaped like a cross between a revolver and a trumpet. He pushed the trigger button and a loud fart sound emanated from the plastic toy. Ayana, all forty years of her, caught my shocked and slightly horrified eye. She didn't quite have the English words for it, so I said it for her: "You, you gave my son a fart gun?" "Yes," she said, leaning back into her couch and starting to giggle, "Yes I did."

Ayana and I laughed and laughed until we both had tears in our eyes. And I knew without a shadow of a doubt: Jesus would have been laughing with us. He would have eaten my friend's lamb meatballs and biryani rice too—three plates, maybe four. He would have graciously received second and third cups of tea and pocketed a few boxes of juice to hand out to kids in the stairway. And he would have laughed his head off at that awful toy. Jesus, who reminded us to live like the birds and the flowers that his Father so desperately loved, would receive what was given to him that day in faithfulness. He would celebrate with those who had hard stories, as an act of resistance in an empire of scarcity.

My son ran around Ayana's small apartment, stuffed full of couches and coffee tables and vases filled with fake flowers. He pushed that trigger until the entire place was filled with the sounds of farts and glee, the room erupting in laughter each time he did it. His smile could have split the cloudy Oregon sky and brought the sun out on us all—he was as pleased as if he himself was the author of all of those rude noises. When I tried to leave the loud and noisy toy at her apartment, accidentally-on-purpose, Ayana slipped it back into my son's chubby little hands. She kissed him on the head and waved to us until we walked out of her sight. I could still hear her giggling as we trudged toward our house around the corner. As my son made fart noises in my ear all the way home, I envisioned my friend smiling at the gift that would keep on giving. And I decided to receive the good news of that terrible toy precisely because it had been given with such great love.

PART TWO

AUTONOMY

O, let America be America again—
The land that never has been yet—
And yet must be—the land where *every* man is free.

LANGSTON HUGHES, "LET AMERICA BE AMERICA AGAIN"

8 ★ LIBERTY

I MET MY FRIEND MARYAN because she lived across the courtyard from us. Whenever I would step onto our tiny concrete back patio with my fussy baby in my arms, Maryan would stick her head out of her upstairs window and wave at me, urging me to come up to her place. There I was usually treated to a steaming piece of fresh bread (her specialty) and a plate of whatever was cooking on her stove. She was from Afghanistan and had only been in the United States a few months, and she was incredibly driven to learn English. She practiced on me constantly while she fed me and held my baby.

One day I noticed a large metal pot in an odd shape on her stove. It was thinner at the bottom, got wider in the middle, and then tapered off into a narrow opening with a lid that was tightened with a special screw. I had never seen anything like it. Maryan explained that she had brought it with her from Afghanistan and that it was one of her prized possessions. I finally figured out that it was a variation on a pressure cooker, using trapped steam to cook food more quickly. I eyed it with suspicion, half afraid it would explode in my face, but it only served to churn out delicious meals, day after day.

A year or two later my church asked the congregation for donations for the refugee ministry they ran. They collected the things resettlement agencies asked for, mainly rice cookers and bus passes. Good, practical items, which I heartily approved of, as well as supplies for expecting parents. People love to help during Christmastime, and this was no different—a few people in the church even went above and beyond, buying several of the must-have items of the season, the electric pressure cookers known collectively as "instant pots." The leader of the refugee ministry showed me the huge closet stuffed full of boxes—not just of rice cookers but also diapers and diapers bags and clothes for babies and toys for kids, and those glorious, luminous instant pots. Did I know anyone who could use one? My mind whirred with the possibilities of being able to help my friends. I had seen the recipes proliferating on Facebook, and I knew these machines were expensive and could work well for my neighbors from other countries. Women who made the same few meals they had eaten growing up, meals that usually required many hours on the stove to make the tough cuts of meat tender. Women who were now busy going to community college, taking care of their families, working jobs. Surely this instant pot could make their lives easier, right?

I delivered the boxes with pride to several of my friends. They all expressed surprise and gratitude. I delivered one to Maryan too. I tried to explain how it worked, that it was a better version of the pot she had brought from Afghanistan. On my phone I showed her a quick YouTube tutorial. We unpacked the gleaming silver-and-black contraption and plugged it in. I was so excited to share it and so sure that it would make her life better and easier.

Perhaps you already know where this story is going. The next few times I visited Maryan, I didn't see the instant pot anywhere. Finally, I asked about it. She waved her hand around her tiny, cramped kitchen. There was simply no room for a machine that big, one that needed to be plugged in and took up valuable counter space. No, she would keep using her pot, the one she had brought from her own country. She loved that pot. Giggling, she told me she had started to call it "the magic pot." Why, I asked? Because everyone in the apartment complex wants to use it, she told me. She would cook her family's dinner on it, and then she would leave it on her front doorstep. A neighbor would pick it up, take it home, and cook her family's dinner. And then she would give it to someone else. Maryan waved her arm toward her window. Everyone wants to use this pot. It is because it is magic, she said. It is because it cooks the very best food, just like our mothers cooked, in a less amount of time.

I left that day thinking about the magic pot and the instant pot. My cultural value of efficiency was at odds with Maryan's value of community. It was the difference between a gleaming "instant" solution for one family and a communal pot that gets shared and used and loved by so many. The magic pot not only worked, but it accrued meaning and value with every meal made inside it. It brought people together. It met the needs of so many in a variety of ways, and it did not need me or my individualized solutions to do it. The magic pot came halfway around the world to cook food that has fed me and that my family and so many others have enjoyed. With its thick metal sides and indestructible life, I have to imagine that Maryan's pot will survive long after I am dead and gone. It's a morbid, if comforting, thought. Some items survive not only because they are sturdy but because they are intricately connected, not to modern progress or innovation but because they are the cornerstone of neighborliness to their community.

With Maryan I truly wanted to make my friend's life easier, but I also wanted to feel better. I wanted a psychological reprieve from the pressure that built up whenever I heard her share stories about her life in her country and when I saw with my own two eyes how hard life was in my own city for her. I wanted to forget about the wars and the state-sanctioned violence that had made it necessary for her to flee her home to save the lives of her children. I wanted to gloss over the complex struggles of starting over in a new country in which a large portion of the population did not want you there, where she and her family were either resented and feared or simply patronized by those with good intentions. But my actual relationship with my actual neighbor forced me to step outside of my bubble. To embrace life—including all of its terrible complexities—just as it really was. A world where one shiny new kitchen appliance could not restore what the locusts had eaten.

★ ★ ★

Autonomy is the right to act, speak, live, or govern as you want without restraint. It is independence. For those who have been imprisoned, it makes sense why freedom is something to long for. It makes sense that Jesus came to proclaim liberty to people who had very little control over their lives, who often lived without knowing where their next meal would come from, their lives governed by the whims of a tiny minority of wealthy and powerful rulers.

But what does it mean when those who are already free start to idolize liberty? It can become a weapon to keep other people down. For those of us who grew up with food in our bellies and a roof overhead and in a place where our skin color and theologies and names were normal, what does it mean to long for a world where we are independent? I've discovered how much I resist having my own selfish desires restrained by the needs and stories of others, especially those for whom the American Dream is only a myth.

My husband likes to say that we need the church to be our recovery group; we need it to be a place where we can share how tempted we are by the values of our world: upward mobility, progress, success, programs, achievements, individuality. I am drawn to these values because I want something to hold in my hand, something I can shove up to the sky and prove to God that I have done something, that I have made a difference, or that I have done well with what I was given. With my own clenched fingers I have saved the world. But the truth is, in this mindset I grow ever more lonely and ever more isolated, both railing against the American Dream and unable to listen to those who have always been creating paths of resistance to the dehumanization of others within the myth we all reside in.

My story would have continued on the lonely path of the free if I hadn't been jolted out of complacency by my neighbors, flesh-and-blood people who ministered to me, taught me, embraced me, confronted me, challenged me, ignored me, and even hated me. My neighbors saved me from myself and from a culture that taught me that at age nineteen I had all the right answers to the mysterious, consuming, burning love of God. They restrained me. Their love allowed me to take small, scared steps into a world that is more broken than I could possibly believe and a faith in the God who will redeem us all. I am and continue to be liberated from my role as the captor with intentions of gold. And God has used my neighbors to pierce through the value of autonomy in my own life.

Several years into our friendship now, Maryan treats me like a younger sister. Recently she noticed the new-to-us car my husband had purchased, a tiny little shiny vehicle with good gas mileage and a cheap price tag. My husband was so proud of this car, a sign of frugality. But Maryan saw it differently. She had multiple children and no driver's license. Going to the grocery store for her was an immense undertaking, especially since we live in what is technically a food desert. Ever since she left her home country she had been denied the simple pleasure of grocery shopping, of touching the food with her own hands. Now, her husband got together with the other men and shopped once a week, using the long lists she wrote as a guide for what the family would eat.

Maryan took one look at our little car and said, "What, did you not think of us when you bought this car?" My heart sank within me, desperate to explain myself, our decision to purchase something that was cheap and reliable and that suited our small family's needs. Maryan shook her head. "For someone with a big heart," she said, "you sure do like small cars." We laughed together, but her honesty was a gift that cut several ways. She was pointing out that we come from different cultures, with different values. My first impulse is usually to take care of myself first. I do not view Maryan's troubles as my own, as my responsibility in the way that families care for one another. I do not buy my food or my clothes or my cars in a way that connects me to the "unescapable web of mutuality." I am lonely in my small car, saving on my gas bill, isolated as I hurtle down the streets to take care of my own personal errands. But friends who cook me good meals and tell the truth about their reality and mine help burst the bubble of my own making, time and time again.

I think about this as I eat yet another meal prepared for me in the magic pot, as I watch Maryan serve me and then prepare to share her bounty with another family. In apartments like hers, I have slowly watched my values change. It hasn't been instant, as much as I would like it to be. And in many ways it still stings. We are never as autonomous as we would like to believe; someone usually pays for our freedoms, as so many have been trying to tell us. And the only way those of us obsessed with freedom can learn a new way of living depends on taking the time to become connected to the real teachers, our neighbors: the ones who feed us from the deep wells of their one experience. The ones who have the keys to truly liberating us all.

9 ⭑ THE NAMES WE GIVE

A YEAR OR SO AGO I WAS ON AN AIRPLANE flying to meet up with a small group of female Christian activists. I was transfixed as the woman next to me took out a small tin filled with squares of chalky paint. She had a clear plastic brush filled with water, and she started to make a tiny replica of the view outside the plane window. She was in the middle seat, so she had to crane her neck past me to get a good view for her work—the light blue sky, the cotton clouds, the red tip of the plane's wing, the rounded oval frame of the window. She noticed my eyes sliding over to her work, and as she painted she started to talk quietly and pleasantly. She spoke of the old friends she was flying to see. Her love of watercolors happened later in life. Her only daughter, now about to graduate from high school. The changing of her life's seasons, the wistfulness of new horizons.

She asked me about my destination. I told her where I was headed, but that I didn't feel like I belonged. I felt like I wasn't good enough for these amazing activist women. The confessions poured out of me, the plane a sacred and separate place, like a confessional booth in the sky. I heard myself telling this stranger that I never felt good enough, not ever, that I was afraid of harming the communities I most wanted to help because of my stubbornly ingrained savior complex, my ever-present desire to be found right. I told her that I was angry because the world was falling apart and scared that by trying to help I was only making it worse.

The woman made miniature brush strokes in blues and grays, dipping her brush into her repurposed box of mints. I have a friend like you, she told me. He started off small: trying not to buy anything with excess packaging, bicycling to work to cut down on carbon emissions. Now, she told me, looking me straight in the eye, now he refuses to buy toilet paper. She paused for a moment. He wipes his ass with his own hand, she said, as if to herself. She shook her head and went back to painting.

I sat quietly, thinking about this admission. I could see my life stretched out in front of me. I could see where all my good works would lead me, crippling me from enjoying the blue of the sky or the white of the clouds. I was tired of trying to pretend I was good, that I could control the chaos of the world with my small actions. But the problem was, I didn't know how to stop.

★ ★ ★

Many of my Muslim friends can tell me, without hesitation, what their name means and how important it is to them. Most of their names have an Arabic root, which means many other people will also know exactly what their name means and even how to interact with them based on their name. Names are useful for positioning people, for understanding them, for helping identify where someone is placed in a community, perhaps even their personality, talents, and abilities.

The American in me still finds this weird. Isn't everyone as unique as a snowflake? Perhaps, but viewed from a few feet away, humans do have similar characteristics and compulsions. My own cultural orientation toward extreme individualism (with an emphasis on being self-made) makes me distrust this belief in names and what they say about us and what they mean for our communities.

My middle name is Louise, after my great-grandmother. I know very little about this woman except that her house was a haven for my mother when she was small and her life was very hard. Great-Grandma Louise had a small house in Kansas that sheltered a girl from the storms of life, and that girl grew up to be my mom. Old-fashioned, archaic, stately: *Louise* is a name to grow into, a name worthy of being carried on.

My first name, Danielle, is the feminine version of Daniel, from the famous Bible story about a prophet and a den full of lions. It is a name that always seemed slightly ugly to me—too many letters and hard to pronounce. When I was a precocious seven-year-old I decided to make my name seem more sophisticated and went around telling anyone who would listen that the origins of my name were French. But really it was Hebrew, straight from the Old Testament; it means "God is my judge." It's a very good name if you are religious, and I have always been a very, very religious soul. I've always been severe, with a mind constantly roiling with questions about how to be good. Over time my name began to accrue meanings that would take decades to unwind.

As a child my nicknames given to me by my family were "the perfect child" and even "the holy spirit." At the time I thought these nicknames were signs of my own goodness; I did not see the saltiness of a little girl who thought she could obtain the perfection of God if only she tried a little bit harder. I twisted the meaning of my name. I concluded that I was a judge. I would scour the Bible for stories of people who had done things right and strive to align myself in their ranks. I never stopped to consider what I was so afraid of. I never stopped to wonder what kind of Judge I was running from.

My name is connected to my story: I grew up idolizing the mostly single missionary women I read about as a child. They were so good, so right, and so very lonely. I believed that my name was mine alone to carry. Naturally, this led me to believe that I alone was responsible for judging the world and therefore for saving it too. My individualism grew in me a classic savior complex: a desperate longing to be of use, coupled with an inability to listen, love, or be transformed by others, especially those I wanted to help. My name became a source of anguish, a reminder of all the ways I was being judged and found wanting because I was viewing things through the lens of an isolated individual. One girl with the whole world on her shoulders—both dangerous and lonely.

One night my husband and I were having dinner with good friends, talking about names. The names of our children and then our own. I confessed that my name reminded me of how judgmental I can be—that it was a source of shame, a spotlight on my true vice. My friend

Zach looked at me incredulously. A Georgia boy with the heart of a Jesuit priest, in his Southern drawl Zach told me I had it all wrong. "Your name means God is the judge, not you," he said. "It means that all the things in the world that make you upset, you can take to God." *If only I could*, I said silently to myself. If only I could give back this great weight on my shoulders. If only I could experience a moment of freedom from the cares of the world.

* * *

Like many Americans I picked the names of my own children because I liked the way they sounded. They also had literary connections since I am first and foremost a reader. My daughter came first and I named her Ramona, after the books by Beverly Cleary. Both so that she would remember her Portland roots (Cleary was born and raised here) and also because I secretly hoped any daughter of mine would be strong, spunky, and not a typical "good" girl. My Ramona has lived up to her name and then some—for years she refused to read the Ramona Quimby books because she was convinced she was nothing like her (a very Ramona response). But I have been pleasantly surprised at how her name has translated well to our friends and neighbors from other cultures. Spanish-speaking friends immediately recognize her name and so do our friends with Arabic names (Mona is a popular choice for women). Her name rolls easily off the tongue of nearly everyone she meets; her name brings joy to so many.

Then there is my son. Ever since I was a teenager and read C. S. Lewis' sci-fi space trilogy, I had been taken with the name of his main character, Dr. Ransom. I made up my mind at a very young age that this would be the name of my son if I ever had one. Now I have a little blond Ransom who delights in all that the world has to offer: Pokémon, ladybugs, sprinklers, and vampires. I love his name because I picked it out—but I wasn't thinking about our wider community. From day one, when we started telling our friends and neighbors what our tiny squishy five-pound baby was named, we got confused looks and scrunched noses. Friends from generational-poverty backgrounds wondered aloud why we didn't just go ahead and name him "felony" or "misdemeanor." Friends from non-English language backgrounds stumbled on the new-to-them word. Recently a teenager who was checking in Ransom to children's church stopped and looked at me. "His name is Ransom?" the teenager asked me, incredulous. "As in, I am going to kidnap your child and hold him for ransom?" "Yes," I said, trying not to laugh. "Exactly like that."

I can laugh about it now, but the names we choose and the way we go about this process speaks to the values of our family background and overall culture. I did not think about the greater community or even what the names I gave my children meant. I liked the way they sounded; they pleased me on an individual level and seemed like strong names for the types of nonconforming adults I would hope they would grow into. But the older they get and the more I see a wide array of people interact with them, the more I realize the power of names. They can invite people in, or they can confuse. I never used to understand why the most popular names in the world are all variations on Mohammed, John, Miriam/Maryan/Mary. But now I see the connections to the stories, to the traditions people long to continue on.

* * *

When she was three, my daughter told me that she didn't like her name anymore. She had decided to change it. "My name is Mohammed," she told me, her face slightly defiant. "No," I said, "it's not." "Yes it is," she insisted over and over again until I asked her why she wanted to change it. "Because," she said, "everyone I know is named Mohammed." I realized then and there how very different a childhood my daughter was having from my own.

Because of our ever-widening circle of neighbors, I realize more and more how our names connect us to stories that are greater than an isolated individual. They speak about family, culture, religion. They carry the threads forward into history, they tie us to one another. I did not think about this when I named my children, and I did not think about this when I felt ashamed of my own name. But slowly, I am starting to see how we can choose to connect with one another, even in the smallest of ways, and the rippling effects of these choices.

Now when my Muslim friends ask me about my name, I have learned to be proud. "Allah is my judge," I will answer them nonchalantly, and usually they squeal *Mashallah!* and clap their hands for me, they are so pleased with my good, strong name. They are so happy to find an American with a name that is also oriented toward God, toward the community. And through their delight I have found my own rigid little heart softening. God, the very good judge, the one who loves my friends and neighbors more deeply than I could ever imagine, also loves me.

On the plane I watched my seatmate take the time to carefully paint the view of the clouds outside our window. I was mesmerized, my fingers itching for my own brush. We were quiet for the rest of the flight, both of us trying in our own ways to not think about the metal plane keeping us alive and buoyant, about all of the small disasters that could happen at any moment. Was she painting a miracle or a distraction? I couldn't decide. I watched her, stroke by stroke, paint what she could see over my shoulder. A world so neatly contained, one I could never touch, and therefore never ruin, with my loving, soiled hands.

10 ✶ FRESH PAINT

THE OTHER DAY I WENT TO AN EVENT in our community designed to "love on" our elementary school. A big sign on the fence said "Love Rockwood." At various events over the summer I had seen people from a church group helping out at community events wearing red visors or hats with the same slogan on them. Those hats and visors, those banners hanging up on the fence during a community project work day, brought up a lot of feelings for me. I felt conflicted—grateful that our elementary school was getting attention, thrilled to see hundreds of people descend onto our little school and give it a new coat of paint, landscape the children's garden, put in fresh-smelling bark chips everywhere. I felt real warmth at the sight of so many busy little bees roaming around the brown August grass, so many men up on ladders, women running the water-and-ice cream stations, the youth group with their goofy leader making balloon animals for the kids in the community.

At the same time I wondered why our school needed to be loved in this way in the first place. Why did it need hundreds of volunteers, most of them White and middle class, to come and do the work of maintaining a pleasing appearance once a decade? Would our school really need this outside intervention, complete with balloon animals and bounce houses and canvas tents and banners, if the people declaring their love actually lived here and sent their children to school here? What exactly does it mean to love a neighborhood, to adopt it, to help it, to fix it, when you wouldn't actually ever move into it?

✶ ✶ ✶

I still remember the way my stomach felt the first time I googled our local elementary school. I knew most of my neighbors sent their children there, of course—beautiful, loud, intelligent, disobedient, belligerent, kind, and shy children. I knew my own value was to live with my neighbors in mind, and that included sending my kids to the same school as they did. But as my daughter neared school age, and I, like so many other parents from my similar background, googled the school to find out more about it, I felt queasy. I felt my values slowly sinking out of my pores. I found myself staring at a large red score of 1, the lowest score on a scale that went upwards to 10. I saw a school that had been deemed a failure. And I feared that I was signing my own child up for failure by sending her there.

I remember gathering up my fizzling resolve and setting up a meeting with the principal. My daughter would be entering the next year, but I wanted to scope it out. I met with the principal and stammered out a few questions. I mentioned I was interested in sending my daughter to school there, and that I wanted to get involved and help the school, help the families. Did they need help? How could I best support them? The principal was busy, he had things to do, and he looked me in the eye and in a few sentences deflated all of my carefully constructed hierarchies. Well, if you want to send your child here, do it, he said. But we already have a lot of great families, and we're all working hard together here. If you want to join us, you're more than welcome.

He smiled brightly in the way that meant the meeting was over. I walked back through the halls of that unassuming building, the walls covered in pastel murals, art projects, and cheerful slogans. I was shocked at the joy I felt, almost as tangible as a mild electric current. I don't know why I was surprised: there in the midst of a large concentration of children and the people dedicated to helping them learn and grow and be safe. Joy—along with outbursts of anger, frustration, curiosity, boredom—was a natural outcome of grouping kids together, of rounding up all of these little humans made in the image of God.

The principal's answer had astonished me. It was exactly the right response, centering the hardworking families of the community and crushing my White do-gooder dreams. I was impressed, and I filled out the enrollment paperwork immediately. When I found out this principal took another job at a better-paying and better-resourced district, I was disappointed. But it was too late. He had already convinced me to join the good work that was already happening. I'm indebted to him for that short conversation we had. In the years that have passed since, I have fallen ever more deeply in love with all of the people that make up our little school, our bastion of light in the midst of a world hell-bent on not investing in certain communities.

★ ★ ★

People have the right to make whatever choices they want about where they live and how they educate their children. This liberty is woven so deeply into our minds we don't know how to interrogate it. We can talk about loving our neighbors all day long, but this can be hard to do when we orient our lives around loving ourselves and our immediate families. We make these choices under the name of common sense, the natural and normal pursuit of achievement and success, and of the God-given commandment to love your children. But what happens when our freedoms affect the freedoms of others?

Perhaps it's time for people like myself to spend more time considering the ramifications of exercising our rights. In my experience, people like me—people with privilege in an unequal society—love to talk about intent. We want to do good. We want to love others. We want to help others (and if it only happens every few years, and a big deal is made of our help, then that's the cherry on top of the cake).

But I'm tired of talking about intent. Instead, I want to talk about impact. I want to talk about what happens when we all choose what we believe is best for ourselves or for our children in a world that's set up for some people to exploit and benefit from inequality. And I can think of no more concrete example of the devastating effects of this pattern than the public education system in the United States.

★ ★ ★

Nikole Hannah-Jones writes almost exclusively on racism in the United States. Like so many who are paying attention, she believes the issue of school segregation lies under the surface of so many other issues. The choices we make in regard to education—both at the policy and individual levels—have ripple effects that go on for decades. In her work Jones focuses on schools in light of the recent history of desegregation in the United States. For years, Black children were segregated into Black schools, White children to White schools. The practice was inherently dehumanizing and contributed to segregation and unequal access to resources, and the Supreme Court found it to be unconstitutional in 1954.

Without forced integration through the court system, we would never have known how well it works for all. The results were plain: it raised both scores and graduation rates for Black children, and it wasn't detrimental to White children, whose scores and graduation rates remained the same.[1] And yet, since the heyday of integration in America in the 1980s and 1990s, we have slowly slipped back into schools that are largely segregated—much like our neighborhoods. While there are few all-White schools left, there are many schools that are all-Black or all minority students. How and why does this happen? The answer is clear: White parents are behind the push to resegregate.

These decisions are couched in many different terms: people just want what is best for their kids. They want to give them the freedom to explore. They want them to get a Christian education. They are worried about godless public schools. They want to make sure their kids grow up with their values. They want more time to be together as a family. They want to protect their kids from the realities of the world as long as possible. And while there are certainly circumstances and individual children that make these decisions more complicated, the majority of privileged parents perpetuate narratives that center on anxiety about scholastics and achievement, religious education, peer friendships, and about protecting one's children from the world. And the impact, regardless of intent, boils down to actions that prioritize individual benefits over the collective flourishing of a community.

All forms of education are political and reflect the beliefs of the caregiver (and society as a whole). We are all experimenting with our children, all the time. All of us influence our children because of our politics—how we engage our responsibility to be civically minded. Those who opt out of the public education system—whether through homeschooling or by immersing themselves in a specific denomination or Christian school or going to great lengths to send their children to an elite private or public school—are also making choices and placing their kids on a different kind of altar: one that assumes that the sacrifice is worth it and that their children need to somehow get ahead in a world where some will be the captors and others will be the captives.

★ ★ ★

Someone's kids have to attend the worst school in your city. In your mind whose kids should that be? I think our answers to that question reveal a great deal about how deeply the American value of autonomy has been lodged in our hearts. We will fight to ensure that our kids get the best, and we try to forget about everyone else—unless perhaps, every once in a while, there's an opportunity for charity, to give back, or to "love on" that fits our needs and maintains the status quo of the hierarchy (and makes us feel better, to boot).

My husband and I chose our daughter's school on purpose, and we have the privilege and social mobility to do so. But school choice is not a reality for the majority of my neighbors. For one, there are few options in our neighborhood—two or three small charter schools that don't reflect the racial or socioeconomic makeup of our neighborhood. When we moved into this neighborhood, my daughter was five. We lived in an apartment complex that was infamous for many reasons, but which we found to be a haven for families from many different backgrounds. We didn't have a single conversation about school choice, although it was a constant topic of conversation for most of my White, middle-class friends who lived elsewhere. All of the neighbors I knew—most of them immigrant and refugee families—weren't trying to get into alternative schools or thinking about homeschooling. It made me wonder why they weren't doing everything in their power to "get ahead." Why weren't they more afraid of the school system, of what it might do to their beautiful, unique children?

But then I realized most of them trusted the system and took it at its word. The United States government said that the mission of the Department of Education is "to promote student achievement and preparation for global competitiveness by fostering educational excellence and ensuring equal access."[2] Some of my neighbors believed in the myth. They believed that what America really wanted was for every child to have the right to a good and equitable education—even as all the evidence suggested otherwise, even as everybody in the know either abandoned or never even set foot in the schools classified as "bad," because of poverty or race, disguised as test scores.

The more we work together in our neighborhood, at our low-rated school, the more we are working at getting more power to the families who are farthest from the seats of decision making. This involves complicated parent-group meetings, uncomfortable conversations, showing up at school board meetings and reaching out to superintendents. It means paying attention to demographics, funneling resources into things that benefit the most children instead of hoarding resources for a few.

As the apostle Paul says, "'Knowledge' puffs up, but love builds up" (1 Corinthians 8:1). Learning for the sake of acquiring more than someone else is the definition of a puffed up education. But loving and building resources into the groups that have historically been disinvested in by both the system and by individuals? That's what it means to love our school and our neighborhood: to build power, starting from the very bottom of the hierarchy. That is what we need more than any once-a-decade event designed to clean up our building.

What does it mean to love something, to "love on" a community when you won't live there or send your kids to school there? It means you only want to love it in a certain way, a way that keeps the world as it fundamentally is, but with a fresh coat of paint every decade or so. I think it's a form of propping up structures of inequality while calling it charity.

The "Love Rockwood" banners and signs and hats still feel jarring to me when I see them. The truth is, I do love our community, our school. So does my daughter. So does the majority of our community. On paper there might be a few concerns, like how the test scores are not great, or how over 94 percent of the student body is at or below the poverty line. But this is what it looks like in the flesh: my daughter eating a free school lunch every day along with her classmates (and sometimes breakfast too). Going to the kind of school where good-hearted people deliver backpacks stuffed full of school supplies or jackets or mittens. Her small body sitting shoulder to shoulder with children who have known (and who continue to know) all sorts of trauma. Together, these children of God are building each other up into the kind of neighbors Jesus envisioned. The ones who have been taught to see differently than the empire sees. The ones who believe that the poor are blessed, that the meek and the overlooked are the ones who'll make the best leaders, and that those who have mourned and suffered will throw the best parties in the new creation.

I still remember the joy I felt the first time I walked those halls, because it comes back to me every time I am inside that space. It's one of the only places in our entire city that treats these precious children as if they are worthy of being invested in. It's one of the only spaces in our neighborhood where anyone, regardless of income, race, able-bodiedness, or religion will be served to the best of the school's ability. While there are still real challenges to be faced in such an unequal system (especially for kids of color), I can't deny the presence of the Holy Spirit; it's obvious to me that our school is a place where God is at work. But love is not just a feeling, not just the spark in my step I get at our school. Love is a concrete way of living in the world that prioritizes others, and other people's children, over our own. Because of my relationships with people who live on the outskirts of the American Dream, I've had the privilege of having my values laid bare before me. I've had to ask myself time and again what my highest value for my family is: Do I want my child to "succeed" in the cultural-achievement oriented sense, or do I want her to succeed at loving her neighbor as herself? Which value is stronger?

My friends and neighbors don't have the resources that the outside church group did—they didn't have the tents or the tractors or the money to buy bark chips. But they love their school every day in the ways that count: braiding their children's hair before school, checking backpacks at night, showing up for school events, cooking a feast from around the world for Teacher Appreciation Week. Most of them have no grand intentions of saving or even "loving on" our neighborhood. They simply live here and understand that we will all benefit when we all flourish. They keep showing up. They teach me about the importance of looking at our impact, loving me and my daughter all the while.

11 ✶ WHAT IS EDUCATION FOR?

I GREW UP WILD AND FREE. Homeschooled, unschooled, I read whatever books appealed to me and spent long hours outdoors letting my imagination wander. I had the kind of education many modern parents look at longingly. I wasn't in public schools at a desk all day learning how to be a pliant citizen or godless liberal. I came out as a model test subject: strong-willed, strong faith, strong test scores. Unconstrained by the shackles of what the majority of children had to undergo. I loved my childhood, and in some ways I have my education to thank for who I am today—my love of reading, my desire to continue learning all the days of my life. But sometimes, when I was a child, I would read books about kids who went to school, and I would wonder: *What would it be like to be surrounded by so many kids? What would it be like to live in a community? What would it be like if school wasn't just about me sitting with a book interacting with an author who died long ago, but was also about learning to be a child in the world full of other, very different children?* Of course, the two values aren't mutually exclusive, but our values about education are strongly influenced by our beliefs about the importance of autonomy versus community.

As a product of the Christian homeschooling movement, our sense of community was quite small: people who believed just like us, a ragged band of nonconformists. We did not feel a sense of responsibility to the wider world and in fact were encouraged to shun it. I think my question now remains this: To what purpose? What does it mean to be wild and free, to long for that for ourselves and for our children, in a world where so many do not have that option?

✶ ✶ ✶

I know we are not supposed to have heroes anymore because they always disappoint us in the end. But there remains in my life someone who I am both dazzled and baffled by, someone who was life-changing because he identified a need before anyone else in the world did, and he addressed that need with the entirety of his life and work. Fred Rogers is a man who has lived out the Christian concept of vocation: using the gifts that God gives us to the fullest extent of our possibility in the world. He was a radical figure, sometimes controversial. He was the gentlest preacher of our lives, dressed in a sweater vest and comfortable sneakers, looking directly into the camera, telling children that they were beloved and accepted just as they were.

Mr. Rogers and his make-believe world was a familiar and soothing presence in my own childhood. But the more I've learned about him, the more I admire his laser-like determination to reach all the children he could with tools for social and emotional intelligence. He was on a quest to tell children that their feelings and lives mattered, that who they were at their core was seen and valuable. And he was also determined to think beyond the traditional rubric of education. In later years his show, *Mr. Rogers' Neighborhood*, was held up and criticized against the more popular and energetic *Sesame Street*, which taught children the ABCs and their numbers. But Fred Rogers remained firm in his commitment to writing episodes that revolved around the feelings and situations that children find themselves in, especially the ones they find scary.

For all of his meek and mild demeanor, Mr. Rogers was driven by a deep-centered desire for what really mattered:

> It's easy to convince people that children need to learn the alphabet and numbers. . . . How do we help people to realize that what matters even more than the superimposition of adult symbols is how a person's inner life finally puts together the alphabet and numbers of his outer life? What really matters is whether he uses the alphabet for the declaration of war or the

> description of a sunrise—his numbers for the final count at Buchenwald or the specifics of a brand-new bridge.[1]

He lived his life in light of the reality of the Holocaust and of Jim Crow laws and of children who were abused and neglected by their own hurting parents. He was angry at what television did for children, how it aimed to pacify them and make them consumers, teaching them to long for material things and gain knowledge without any guidance about its purpose. And so he made his show, and lived a life of ministry, to help children see themselves as God does: as beloved and as people capable of creating a neighborhood where everyone can flourish.

I think about the neighborhood he created, with its trollies and animal puppets finding a home in the trees. It's a tiny symbol of the kingdom of God, of God's dream for the world. It makes me ask myself, *What is education for?* The answer to this question might very well determine how we go about orienting our entire lives and the lives of the people in our care.

For many parents, whatever values they might claim to espouse (character formation, socialization, community building) are eclipsed by their actual motivation: achievement and success as defined by a number of variables: good grades, good test scores, good college, good job. Richard Weissbourd, a Harvard psychologist, studies what he calls a "rhetoric gap." His research suggests that what matters most is not what we say we value to our children but how we act. Out of ten thousand students surveyed, Weissbourd and his colleagues found that almost 80 percent chose achievement or happiness as their highest value, while only 20 percent chose caring for the community. Around 80 percent of those surveyed said their parents cared more about achievement and personal happiness for their children than caring for others in their community or school.[2]

At some point in my life I realized that I do not want what is best for my children—at least not the way *best* is defined by the upwardly mobile White middle class. I think about how "wild and free" is currently a new catchphrase of the unschooling movement, this value of autonomy carefully packaged for the next generation in various Instagram-worthy posts. Sometimes I catch glimpses of these types of images as I scroll through social media: blond-haired children wearing gauzy white dresses gathered at the table in open-concept kitchens, studying Latin or identifying various flora or fauna. I have to admit there was something inspirational about these pictures, something I wanted for myself and my children. But as I clicked through photo after photo I realized they didn't reflect the reality of the majority of the world. They didn't look like many—if any—of the children I knew.

I knew some kids who were having a near-picture-perfect childhood. But I also knew kids who didn't have food at home in the cupboards. I knew kids who had their entire families taken from them. Kids who had been abused or who watched their pets die of starvation or whose parents took too many drugs and drank too much. Kids who showed up to school in a taxi cab—a sure sign that they had just entered the system. Kids whose families were trying so hard but simply couldn't stay afloat. Kids whose parents were doing a better job than what their own parents had given them. Kids who were thriving in situations that would have beaten me down—thriving in places of scarcity and neglect. Kids who could be loud and brash and silly and defiant and disrespectful and hilarious and studious and curious and kind. Kids who were learning multiple languages, multiple cultures, kids who maintained their childlikeness even as they were forced to grow up so quickly. Kids who translated for their parents in all kinds of situations and languages. Kids who invented games and shared their bikes and tried to make sense of all that they were experiencing, kids who worked hard to self-regulate.

Statistically, my neighborhood has the youngest average age in the state—bursting with families, mostly in a cluster of large apartment complexes. There are kids everywhere, most of them living at or below the poverty line. The lines have been drawn so that our school takes the kids from three of the largest apartment complexes, which means lower-income families are concentrated there. Because we don't have community centers and few public parks, the schools are our lifeline to community: the place we interact with each other nearly every day. Our lives revolve around the rhythms and schedules of school—walking to and from, in rain or shine, kissing our children as they rush off to another chaotic and safe day of learning not just how to read but how to live side by side with one another.

I no longer desire to be wild and free—nor do I want this for my children. In my own heart I hear the Holy Spirit working in the opposite ways, asking me to consider making myself responsible for the flourishing of my neighbors. To see the belovedness of them all—every single child in every single school—and to feel the weight of that love. The more I walk the streets of my neighborhood, the more people I get to know, the less wild my thoughts become. I am calmed and restrained by a life where my own liberation is bound up in the flourishing of all.

My daughter sometimes watches *Mr. Rogers' Neighborhood*, just like I did. Her body stills while she watches because she knows she is in safe hands. She's in the presence of someone who knows what it is like to go through life feeling so many conflicting emotions: joy and anger and anxiety and sadness. Even though she is older now, in the third grade, she still loves this man and the way he carefully explains the world around her. She breathes deep and slow while she watches him. And when she turns off the TV and reenters her world, a world full of differences and delights she is only beginning to experience, she has a little better sense of who she is. She is the only one of her in the world, she is beloved just as she is, and she is an important part of her neighborhood. Is there any better education I could hope for?

12 ✶ PAYING ATTENTION TO MY NEIGHBORS

Prayer consists of paying attention.

SIMONE WEIL

A FEW DAYS AGO a neighbor gave my husband and son a brown paper bag full of cherries. Her tree sits outside the small gates that surround her yard. As the school year neared its end, we would walk past—the mothers and the children—and look up at the branches heavy with bright orange and red cherries, not quite ripe enough yet.

My husband happened to be walking by at a lucky moment, and this neighbor, an older woman, offered my husband the bag. When he came home and gave it to me, I frowned. What about everybody else? Why should I accept a gift when there are so many others in the neighborhood who would love to feast?

This morning I took the cherries and pitted them, one by one. I was listening to *The Brothers Karamazov* on audiobook. It's a book about loving your family and loving your neighbor with all of your crooked little heart. It might also be a little bit about being angry at God and wondering at the mess of a world God left for us to muddle through. As I listened I mixed the cherries with sugar and lemon zest and topped it with a lumpy, runny batter. I knew that later we would eat a dessert we did not dream of, one that we did not earn.

I walk around my neighborhood and take notes inside my head. The neighbors who live behind us seem to operate some sort of mechanic shop. There are so many balding, sweating, red-shouldered men. There used to be an old yellow Labrador who wandered around, but I never see him anymore. I wonder if he died. There's a black truck that has been parked there for ages, the faint scrawls of a Confederate flag visible on the rear window with soap or marker. Today there's a new car in the yard, a white sedan with antennas sticking out of the top. In a previous life it had obviously been a police car. The front window has a bullet hole and attendant spider webs of cracks spinning outward. The back windshield has been shot to pieces, glass still scattered over the back seat. When I walked my kids past the house to the elementary school to get the free summer lunch there, they didn't say anything about the car. Children always notice so little and yet so much.

Another neighbor brought her kids over to play this afternoon. They woke my son up from his nap, and he was sweaty as he sat in my lap and started to get used to being awake. The kids ate watermelon outside until they were covered with sticky juice, and then the wasps started to chase them. My neighbor has grown up in generational poverty in the United States, and she told me sad stories of her life. I let them flow over me like water, but some of it escapes into my blood. I know that at night I will turn over the stories I hear, over and over again. My neighbor is a better mother to her children than her mother was to her. She is a miracle if I choose to see it.

In *The Brothers Karamazov*, Ivan (the smart one, who does not believe in God) tries to explain to his brother Alyosha (the good one, who longs to be a monk) that he cannot believe in God because the world is so full of suffering. He tells terrible story after terrible story. He is like me, someone who is forever collecting these snippets of suffering, trauma, and sadness. If you live in the right neighborhoods, if you read the right books, you will find more than you can bear. I imagine Ivan has that wounded look in his eye, that look I have seen in the faces of friends who were born in places like Syria or Somalia, friends who were born into poor and dysfunctional families in the United States, the faces of people who have visited, even for a brief while, the edges of the empire, where things are so obviously unwell. I have seen people look at me with something like desperation in their eyes. So much suffering. So many children discarded, used, and killed.

How could God allow this? I love these friends, just like I love Ivan. They ask the questions because they truly believe that if God exists, then God must be love. And if God is love, then God must also be a perpetual wound, a weeping mother, ever attendant at the funerals of those who die in disgrace and ignominy. If God is love, then God is obsessed with all of these sad stories too.

I asked my neighbor if she liked cherry cobbler, and she said she did. We ate it together on my couch as our children ran and played. She said she liked that it wasn't overly sweet, that there was a tartness to it. She got up to leave. She was going away to another state and didn't know whether she would return. I said I would pray for her. I thought about the famous line from indigenous Australian writer and activist Lilla Watson, "If you have come to help me, you are wasting your time. But if you have come because your liberation is bound up with mine, then let us work together."

I think about all the years of trying to save people, drowning in loneliness, disconnected from the love of God. Now, my are eyes trained toward growing in solidarity, in mutuality, in slowing down enough to listen and sit with—to be a witness to the work of God in a very broken world feels miraculous. Walking around my neighborhood, committing to seeing all my neighbors in all of their complexities and chaos and minor miracles. Sticking around long enough to see the blossoms turn into cherries, to walk the sidewalks long enough to have a bag thrust in our hand, to be safe enough for stories to pour out on our couch, to be there still when people come back from travels if they ever do at all.

This is what it means to pray these days: to watch the cherries slowly ripen and to listen to the stories of suffering big and small. To put down roots in order to see the seasons engage their miraculous rebirth continually, to lament that the world is not how it should be. The cherry cobbler was delicious, but it didn't fix anything. Still, I savored it as best as I knew how. I'm learning to take the sweet moments as I get them, not knowing how long they'll last.

13 ✶ THE HOSPITALITY OF EXILES

We
Who do not own ourselves, being free,
Own by theft what belongs to God,
To the living world, and equally
To us all

WENDELL BERRY

Every time I drive past an apartment complex, I feel an ache in my chest because I do not and cannot live there. Do other people experience this? The desire to know what life is like in all the little corners of the world, to make a home in the hidden-away spaces where people are crammed into proximity to each other? I've lived in several different apartment buildings as an adult, and my recollections are all dreamy: sunlight filtering through windows, inviting neighbors into my space and being invited into theirs, crossing cultural and racial and socioeconomic boundaries, receiving the gift of a diverse community.

My husband remembers it differently. He reminds me that in certain seasons we were so busy we were like ghosts, slight impressions in the microcosm of life in a complex. Other times we were frightened by the sounds of our neighbors screaming in rage, wailing in sorrow, taking their fights out into the corridors, people in a mental health crisis, and people trying to wash away their sadness with gallons of vodka or pipes full of hard drugs. The sickly sweet smell of passing out, of numbing out, of trauma breaking through. Or the nights when neighbors would sail into our apartment without knocking when our small living room was another extension of the outdoors—so little privacy, all exposed, no respite for the introverts, constant invitations into spaces and feasts and stories.

When my husband reminds me of these experiences, I can start to remember the nuances. But it all goes out the window as I drive slowly past a complex, full of peeling paint and mothers bouncing babies on their knees, a big sign saying "Now Accepting Applications." I want to live there; I want to sit around and see how people go about their lives; I want to become a known entity, benign as a mailbox, a staple of the community, a watchful grandmother. I want to do this in every apartment complex in America. I want to know and be known by every person who lives in these spaces that cater to those working very hard to make it. That's not too much to ask, is it? Sometimes I tell this to my husband, and he just shakes his head at me. "Danielle," he says, full of kindness, full of wisdom. "You can't be neighbors with everybody. You can only be a good neighbor to a few. So pick those neighbors on purpose."

★ ★ ★

I once read that *philoxenia*, the Greek word for hospitality, means "love of the stranger." Much of the hospitality shared on my social media feeds is geared toward family, friends, and church groups. Oftentimes it revolves around conversations about immaculately decorated houses or complicated recipes pulled off with aplomb. It is about a hostess with killer hair and a cozy house. For some it's just a way of expressing themselves; for others, those already drowning in bills, in children, in an inability to get out of bed to tidy up, this kind of hospitality is a millstone around their neck.

There's a story about a woman who put a picnic table in her front yard, painted it turquoise blue, and sat at it until she started meeting some of her neighbors. She wrote a book about this table, colored the same shade that a multitude of Christian inspiration books also mysteriously flaunt. The turquoise table is not a bad idea, not at all. It was a bold move to break free from the isolation that the American suburban experience is built on. It was one woman making a claim that the dream was too narrow for her. She needed a flag, a bright turquoise one, that she could plant as a sign that there was more to life than the kingdom she was building inside. She sat at the table and invited others to join her, and relationships were forged.

This woman reached out to the strangers around her, and it resonated with her audience of other people who I assume also felt that same pull toward neighborliness. But is it true hospitality, I wonder? Does it really get to what the love of the stranger really means? In order to love the stranger we have to love the people who are the most estranged from us. And that would involve upending the entire system, how neighborhoods and shopping centers and schools and churches are all built by people wanting to be with those who are just like them. A turquoise table simply won't reach far enough if the people in your neighborhood are the result of targeted systems of segregation. A turquoise table will not do if your suburb—your neighborhood—is built on the backs of the people being excluded.

Xenophobia is the opposite of hospitality. In Greek, it means "the fear of the stranger." It's in the very air we breathe: it's built into our mortgage contracts, our constitution, our foreign policy, our immigration system, and the speeches that elect our politicians. It's the large backyards and the white picket fences, the parents googling a school's rating and buying houses based on the result, Facebook groups casting judgment on "suspicious" males wearing hoodies, police brutality that disproportionately affects Black and Brown people, locking our car doors as we drive through a neighborhood we have no curiosity about. The fear of the other is so strong and so systemic that it might take something more than a good dinner party to upend it.

★ ★ ★

In a famous passage the Catholic mystic and monk Thomas Merton writes about seeing a vision of God's love. He was struck with an invisible lightning bolt from the divine. There's even a plaque, I am told, in the town square in Kentucky where he had his vision:

> In Louisville, at the corner of Fourth and Walnut, in the center of the shopping district, I was suddenly overwhelmed with the realization that I loved all those people, that they were mine and I was theirs, that we could not be alien to one another even though we were total strangers. It was like waking from a dream of separateness, of spurious self-isolation in a special world, the world of renunciation and supposed holiness. The whole illusion of the separate holy experience is a dream. . . . And if only everybody could realize this! But it cannot be explained. There is no way of telling people that they are all walking around like the sun.[1]

He goes on to write that monks live in the same broken world, the world of the atomic bomb, of race hatred, mass media, technology, and so on. The difference is that monks are conscious that they belong to God, but the truth is—everybody belongs to God. Why should they consider themselves different or better? "Thank God, thank God," he wrote, "that I am like other men, that I am only a man among others."

Born and raised in suburbs or semirural areas, I did not grow up viewing my neighbors walking around as bright as if they were the sun. The stereotypical wave and smile was the norm, especially as my family moved every two to three years. But the exceptions stand out vividly. When I was a senior in high school my mother made me check on our elderly neighbor nearly every day. "Make sure she's still alive," my mom would cheerfully tell me as she pushed me out of the house. I would knock on Marguerite's door, and I can still remember the prayers I prayed, "Oh Lord, help me not to be the one to discover her body. Please let today not be that day."

It never was that day, thankfully. Instead, I got an education in neighborliness, both the awkwardness and the blessing of it. Marguerite, who was in her late eighties, was like no one I had ever met. She was what my parents would have described as a liberal—the radio constantly tuned to NPR, the *New York Times* always perched next to her chair. Her house was mostly books and houseplants. I don't remember what we chatted about, but it mostly revolved around books. My parents would invite her over for Christmas and she would come, sitting somewhat stiffly through all of our prayers. When I left home for new adventures, Marguerite gave me an ornate brocade chair and a broken uke-banjo (half ukulele and half banjo). Delightful, completely impractical gifts from a woman who gave me a glimpse into an alternate way of living. Surrounded by knowledge, surrounded by the world, and yet still capable and desiring of community.

But sometimes we need help to swim against the current of isolation that moves beneath our way of living. My friend Breanna lives half the world away in Southeast Asia. She upended her life to be a learner. She writes beautifully about how living in cramped, close quarters, with all of her neighbors knowing everything about her business, has enabled her to see the loneliness of the American landscape when she returns home for a visit. Everyone with their houses in the suburbs, their garages, their swing sets in the backyards. They are alone, Breanna realizes now, and they don't even know it. She tries to explain this to her neighbors in Southeast Asia, and they are shocked that most people in the United States don't know their neighbors. They feel sorry for us.

My neighbors born in other countries have communicated the same to me many times over. When we moved into our current neighborhood we were warned about the crime rates by outsiders. And while some things were hard to get used to—including celebrations that went into the wee hours and a neighbor who confused the gas pedal with the brakes and drove his car into my daughter's bedroom—overall we felt incredibly safe. It was a space filled with people who had not grown up with the dominant culture values of autonomy and privacy. We found there is immense safety in community, in knowing people. And the opposite is also true: fear laces all of our privacy and autonomy, a fear that comes from being estranged from the people in our neighborhoods.

When I drive around neighborhoods with large homes and spacious yards, I feel a rush of questions: How do people pay for those huge spaces? How do they reconcile having that much room, that much stuff with the realities of other people in our city struggling to pay the water bill, while the shelters are stuffed to overflowing with homeless families? But there's also a sense that this loneliness is on purpose, though we never say this aloud. That we believe people are supposed to be affluent, and they are supposed to be autonomous—even if it turns out to be very bad for their souls.

There's a reason my heart leaps within me whenever I see another large, battered apartment complex with a sign proclaiming a room for rent. There's a reason I want to move in there, immediately. It's because these are some of the very few spaces in our country and our culture where interdependence is a necessity, where it is a discipline that can be cultivated. These apartment complexes mirror the world of the biblical writers, who would be baffled by how individualism, consumerism, and affluence have shaped our communities—including how we live, eat, shop, educate our children, and worship.

Just like affluence, autonomy can be hard to see unless we are given a different perspective through relationship and education and the Holy Spirit working in our hearts. As we learn how to live in community and how to retain our dependence on one another, we were also inadvertently learning how to navigate a world that will never be completely safe but is full of people shining like the sun—if only we have eyes to see.

PART THREE

SAFETY

No one leaves home unless
home is the mouth of a shark
you only run for the border
when you see the whole city running as well

WARSAN SHIRE

14 ✶ THE ODDS

My father is obsessed with Shark Week on the Discovery Channel. He finds the entire debacle both hilarious and strangely exciting, watching those magnificent, graceful, terrifying sea monsters roam their underwater kingdoms. He laughs at how built-up the tension is, how a TV station tries to milk the fears of the public to pay their bills. But he still watches, and sometimes I watch with him.

I am afraid of sharks. I am also afraid of the water in general, never having been a strong swimmer. As a child I always dreaded the clammy feel of seaweed attaching itself to my feet in a lake. I always imagined dead fish squelching in every step I took in mud and muck. There's something about not being able to really see into the water that scares me the most. We fear what we cannot see, what we cannot control. And sometimes we fixate on certain illogical fears in order to avoid facing a reality that has the capacity to do us, and others, much more harm. There's a saying to illustrate this truth that goes something like this: we fear sharks instead of mosquitoes. And yet, on an average year, sharks kill less than six people worldwide (more people die from their refrigerators falling on them) while mosquitoes kill on average over two hundred thousand people a year. But a dark looming shape in the gloom of water is much easier for our brains to fear than a tiny little bug carrying a virus that can prove fatal.

There is no mosquito week on Discovery Channel. I think this is because malaria is not a threat to most people in the continental United States due to the toxic chemicals we sprayed decades ago. It's not a threat that affects our children, clutched in our hands. It is a threat that kills other people's children, poor children, Black and

Brown and Asian children. Children we don't care as much about as our own, and we are not made to feel bad about this.

★ ★ ★

There is a reason an entire culture can choose to fixate their collective fears on vaccines or terrorist attacks or sharks. While all of these categories do contain some risks, the fear and paranoia are not relative to the actual odds of something bad happening. It's similar to the logic I hear when certain groups of people love to tell me how dangerous immigrant and refugees are to the United States. It's a convenient way to blame an outside group for the anxieties we carry within.

When distant friends and family members post meme after meme on Facebook about the horrors that Muslim refugees are supposedly committing in Europe—how they're hell-bent on coming here and killing people (or perhaps just taking jobs and welfare), how we need to take care of our own first—there's no real way to argue. People who share and promote ideas that demonize entire groups of people are not interested in sharing truth—they're interested in peddling fear. And it works, wonderfully, for those who sell it. It wins them a semblance of control and certainty over their life, and it shores up the boundaries of who is a part of the in-group and who is not. It also wins elections, tipping the balance of power to the one who already has it but who is capitalizing on the fear of losing it.

I understand this because I am a part of it too. Humans long to have an easy answer to the complex problems of the world, and I am among them. My way of dealing with the tension is to tell anyone within listening distance than immigrants are a blessing. After all, I have spent a third of my life both living with and being blessed by refugees, many of them Muslims. I can point to economic evidence—our economy depends and runs on immigration continuing. Or I can bring up the moral argument—we have a responsibility to help resettle people at the forefront of human rights abuses and those escaping the trauma of war and extreme poverty. Or I can go the theological route, hauling out verse after verse where God commands his people to look after the stranger and the foreigner among them. But sometimes I get tired of trying to convince my fellow citizens of the humanity of God's children born someplace else. Sometimes I just want to take a step back and point to the bigger picture. To swivel the heads of those around me in order for them to look at the mosquitoes, as it were, all around us instead of quaking in front of the image of a wide, sharp-toothed shark.

If you live in the United States, you have a 1 in 6 chance of dying from heart disease, and a 1 in 7 chance of dying from cancer. You have a 1 in 88 chance of dying by suicide. You have a 1 in 96 chance of dying from an opioid overdose (a statistic that is on the rise and will continue to grow), a 1 in 103 chance of being killed in a car crash, and a 1 in 285 chance of being killed by a gun assault.[1]

All these statistics have factors that make them more complicated, of course. You are more likely to die in a car crash, for instance, if you actually own a car and drive it most days. But overall, these numbers are a data-driven picture that can help clear the fog from our eyes, if only for a moment. When I take a moment to meditate on these numbers, to stop and consider my own demise and of those around me, a few thoughts float to the surface. Reflections on how our bodies decay, how our brain chemistry betrays us, and our technological advances have unseen and hidden consequences.

I see a despairing sadness in our national discourse on safety. In recent years, as political rhetoric has become more blatantly racist, xenophobic, and Islamophobic, I have seen the language used to talk about immigrants in general and Muslim refugees in particular twisted by fear. When Donald Trump was campaigning for the presidency, and indeed even after he got elected, he liked to recite a poem about a snake that bit and killed the woman who tried to help it. He liked to make comparisons between the snake and Syrian refugees who were fleeing a desperate situation and longing for a place to start over. He called

Mexicans rapists and talked incessantly about Latin American gangs like the MS-13 and their brutal methods of extracting compliance or revenge. He would pull grieving parents on stages and give them microphones—but only if their children had been killed by immigrants.

As much as it concerns me that a prominent leader would do these things, what is more depressing are the crowds at these events. Men and women, mostly older, mostly White, faces set in stony anger or joyous exaltation. They clap for this language, the words that mirror what is in their own hearts. The threat is outside; the threat is another person. The threat is a Syrian woman, a scarf on her head, a child on her hip. She is not a precious person made in the image of God. She is a snake in disguise, waiting to strike. She is an infestation (language that all genocides start with, it should be noted). The Syrian refugee woman is vermin, coming to take jobs and resources, coming to take what should be yours. She is a sad story, to be sure, but we cannot help all of them, the overwhelming hordes of need. Americans—the real Americans—have our own families to think of. We have a commitment to safety and responsibility. We are only doing what is wise, what is necessary.

I cannot watch very many of these political rallies aimed at stoking fear and shoring up power, but sometimes I feel compelled to. My ignorance, after all, will not make my neighbors—especially those who are immigrants, refugees, nonnative English speakers, non-White, nonmale—any safer. But one question remains as I listen to the rhetoric, none of it new or even especially unique to my country. It's the same old song, and it's one that my own mind still quietly sings sometimes when I look at the crowds at the rallies proposing to make American great or to put it first. It's the song that seduces nearly all of us, at some point or other in our lives. It's the song that says we will only be safe or happy or at rest if certain types of people ceased to exist.

One of my favorite poets is Padraig O'Tuama, an Irish man who has seen his share of conflict in his life. "Peace that comes through the annihilation of the enemy," he says, "is no peace at all."[2] O'Tuama warns his listeners to beware of the seeds of eradication that are planted in our own hearts. They love to grow in our troubled soils. I see this principle at work in my own community, which overwhelmingly voted not just for a president but for his policies promising to make America great, safe, and secure—and free from the threat of outsiders. This line of thinking seems practical, but we need to follow the fear all the way to its logical conclusion. Why not hang all of our hopes for safety on banning refugees, on limiting immigration from non-European countries, or building a giant wall at the Mexican border? Why not bomb all Muslims out of existence? Why not eradicate all of those who look like they fit the prototype of a terrorist, a threat to our well-being?

I know this is real because I feel it myself. When I look at a president who almost gleefully twists the narrative of women and children who have suffered at the hands of oppression—when from a stage he calls them snakes and serpents and vermin and refuse—I have the same feeling deep within. Wouldn't my life be better, simpler, and easier if everyone who hated my beloved neighbors simply didn't exist anymore? The seed of eradication lives within me too, though I don't want to admit it. In truth it is behind many of our most basic drives for safety and security, for wellness and greatness.

Like everybody else in my country, I have a 1 in 3.6 million chance of being killed in a terrorist attack by someone who is not a US citizen.[3] It is so far-fetched that to waste any amount of time worrying about it is almost an affront to God and the life that God so freely gives to us. But I have an almost 100 percent chance of dehumanizing others, of wishing them to cease to exist, of longing for the death of others in order to feel safe and secure and happy.

Jesus knows what it's like to move through the world knowing full well that some of our neighbors hate our other neighbors. Jesus knew this, and yet he still asked us to love God and to love our neighbors as ourselves. I recognize I write this from a position of privilege—the power differential between me and a woman from Syria experiencing forced migration is enormous—and Jesus was aware of this too. We can uproot the seeds of hateful eradication within our own hearts while still holding power accountable and still demanding true righteousness, which is justice for the oppressed. We can commit to rid ourselves of dehumanizing others and call out every friend, family member, and neighbor who uses language or rhetoric designed to instill fear or hatred in another.

I used to fear the things hiding in the murk of water. The decay that swirled around, the shark lurking in the shadows seeking to devour me. But evil is real, and it takes on a much simpler form in our world. It is in the cancer that kills us, the car accidents that snatch away the years. And it is also in the fear that seizes our hearts.

There's a greater evil within us than without: the evil of believing and acting on our fear of other people. The notion that if we eradicate the right people, people made in the image of God, we will be secure. The sharks are not the ones that will get us. It is the belief that we can somehow strong-arm our way into safety—that our means, no matter how violent, are acceptable because our own safety is worth all of the harm it brings to others. This is what we should fear: what our own desperate desire for safety might end up doing to those who are beloved in the eyes of God, whom we so carelessly call snakes and sharks.

15 ✶ MARY, OR, WE CAN NEVER BE SAFE

When my son wakes up from his nap, he runs to me and sits close and snuggles for minutes that stretch as long as I can make them. Sometimes we grab a blanket. As he slowly returns to the land of the living, his hair mussed on one side and his cheeks pink from the hard work of growing while he sleeps in his small bed in the corner of his room, he starts to want to play. Sometimes we make a small fort out of that one blanket and our bodies on the couch. We put our heads under the blanket, and that is enough for him. It's magic, the way the light filters through a soft gray fabric. It's me and him, our breath close together, in a world we created. Sometimes I will myself to remember this moment for the rest of my life. I know I won't, which is why I am writing this down right now.

I had a brother who died when I was a baby. Jonah was four years old, almost five. Our entire family—my mother and father, my brother, my older sister, and me—were in a car accident, and my brother was killed. I only know my brother through stories and pictures and through the birthday cheesecake we ate every December 6 to remember him.

In my mind Jonah is the golden boy of our family. He was beautiful, just like my son is beautiful. When he died, so too did my parents' golden world. Now they would go through life as those who had buried their son much too soon. I would grow up with an absence that was permeated with love. It wasn't until I had my own son that I began to recognize the power of my brother's absence. My son showed me afresh all the bright and terrifying possibilities of the future and all the ways it could never fully be in my control.

My brother died in the 1980s, before the ubiquity of video cameras, before we had even dreamed of smartphones. My parents have no video of Jonah, so there is no way for me to hear the sound of his voice or to see how the light moved on his hair. He is not on this earth, and like so many before and after him, there are no statues or monuments to the perfect image of God that he was. My mother and father kept the cards that well-meaning Christians sent them after my brother died. Some of them were terrible in their meaning-making—"when God closes a door he opens a window"—and others were too sad to know what to write, leaving a sympathy card blank save for the scrawl of a name at the bottom. But the card that my mother never forgot, the only card that gave her any iota of comfort, she once told me, was a tiny card that said simply, "God knows what it is like to lose a son."

God knows what it is like to let his precious beloveds wander a world that is not safe, not for anyone. Sometimes, when my son and I are under our blanket whispering silly jokes to each other, enjoying the world we have created, I think about my brother, and then I think about my mother. She might have done this very same thing; she might have experienced this exact moment. The thought fills me with loneliness. All of us will have to experience this, the loss of our children growing up, growing away, perhaps even unto death. We are all in the same boat; we all have to die and so do the ones we love. But most of us spend an awful lot of time trying to convince ourselves it isn't true.

We can never be safe, but oh how we try. I remember when my younger sister got into essential oils. She would breeze into a room, the enchanting scent of spices and citrus wafting in with her flowing dresses and her long, luxurious hair. She was a tornado of good smells and advice on how to use oils to keep my children from getting sick at school and to help them sleep at night. She told me constantly to use oils on my feet, at pulse points, to cure headaches and anxiety and depression. One day I did buy some oils on sale at the discount grocery store, and I even used a little contraption to diffuse them around my house. My own space started to feel better. I would breathe in the scents of clove and tea tree and eucalyptus and lavender, and I would feel as though I had taken back the tiniest bit of control over my life. Maybe today I would not wake up sad. Maybe my daughter wouldn't get the flu. Maybe I could protect us today.

I proudly texted my sister about the oils wafting through my home, carried along by a cloud of diffused air and water. She instantly wrote back, "What brand are they?" I told her I didn't know, I picked them up for a few bucks, which I was also proud of. She quickly texted me back that unless the oils I used were a specific, organic, and expensive brand, then I was most likely poisoning myself and my children with every cancerous, carcinogenic oil droplet we breathed in. I laughed because otherwise I would have screamed. But so often this is the way it goes: the ways we go about pursuing safety don't always work, and sometimes they place an even heavier burden on those who are already struggling.

Eula Biss is a writer who explores this idea in her intriguing book on vaccines called *On Immunity*.[1] She traces not only the history of vaccinations—the inoculations against disease that have transformed our world—but also the modern responses to them. Biss started exploring vaccines when she realized that her community—White, middle-class, highly educated women living in the Upper Midwest—were all having anguished discussions about vaccines. Many of them feared the (relatively minuscule) risks associated with the mandated vaccines, but the conversation never veered into the effects their individual choices to opt out would have on the community as a whole.

Biss interacts with the story of Achilles, whose mother wanted to protect him and keep him safe from the gods. She dipped him in the River Styx when he was a baby, dangling upside down in her hand. But of course, where she clutched at his ankle became the one part of his body that would now be exposed to weakness, so that in a way her attempt to save him contributed to his demise.

In our culture we value a mother's love—or at least certain expressions of it (much of it is based in racial and class preferences that idolize White middle-class sensibilities). For instance, there is a certain motherly panache to declaring how one never gives their children foods with sugar or preservatives or colored dye or never lets them rot their brains with TV or video games. I myself have marveled at such mothers, inwardly fluctuating between wanting to give them a medal and wanting to pity how extra hard their lives seem. And this can extend to how we value our children—their safety and their well-being—and are expected to prioritize them over everyone else.

And yet vaccines are the perfect example of the dire consequences that can occur when people of privilege choose to idolize the safety of their child over the safety of another. It is an example of how those who are the most well-educated can sometimes forget their responsibility to others. Vaccines work and operate successfully based on the logic underneath what is commonly referred to as the "herd immunity." When enough healthy people are inoculated against a disease, they can surround and protect the most vulnerable members (who perhaps can't risk the vaccine) from the encroaching sickness. The healthy take a small risk in order to protect those who need it the most, but what happens when the healthy opt out? When people who are otherwise healthy claim they cannot stomach the risks? When people of privilege choose to value their own safety over the common good, it is the most vulnerable in the community who will suffer, as they always do.

And yet antivaccine sentiment continues to proliferate to this day. Every few months a once-vanished disease makes its way back into schools systems, endangering the vulnerable because of the cultural fixations and fears of parents who have been groomed to believe they can and must save their precious children from every hint of risk. But in their illusions of safety and control lie seeds that will grow up to damage others; by trying to save themselves they harm another.

The myth of safety and wellness continues to unspool around us, one more example of how humans love to create theories and theologies about why some people get sick and others don't, why some get well and others die, and our own roles in keeping the ones we love alive, safe, well, and happy.

* * *

When I had my own son, nearly thirty years after my brother died, I was startled by how much I thought of Jonah. As my son grew older into the sturdy toddler years, I started dressing him in clothes that were a few decades old. I let his hair grow out long and cut it into the bowl cut I remember from the pictures of Jonah I had grown up studying. My son's blond hair and snub nose would catch my eye in the rearview mirror as I drove around to various errands. Sometimes I would catch my breath: that's Jonah in the backseat. Of course, it wasn't. But maybe, just maybe, there is a shadow of my brother in there or at least the love and memory that compels me to keep him present, to keep him alive.

My son was born four weeks early because my body was failing me. He was fine, but I was not, and I spent the first weeks of his life hooked up to machines, willing my heart not to burst, angry at a God who had given me so many precious things to love that I was now terrified to die. All the things I had thought would comfort me in my darkest hour did not help a whit: thoughts of heaven, Bible verses about trusting in God, a tangible presence of the loving arms of Jesus around me. Instead, I felt an almost desperate longing to survive. I wanted to sink my fingers into the earth and stay here forever.

I did not die, but a few weeks after I was released from the hospital my son became the patient, terrifying us all with a meningitis scare at three weeks old. He was so tiny and it was so hard to comfort him with all the tubes and monitors and beeping sounds, day and night. His suffering, his fever, was the final straw that snapped whatever faint illusion of control I had. In the hospital I would go to the room reserved for parents of sick children and eat Lucky Charms slowly out of a Styrofoam bowl. I would glance around at the families, wondering what their sad story was. My son would be fine, we would be out of the hospital as soon as he stabilized, but what about everyone else? In a room filled with light and people getting coffee and talking in hushed voices, I finally felt a little less alone. Here is a room of people who are being forced to grapple with the questions no one ever wants to ask. Here is a room where I didn't have to pretend like I was fine with this system, where everything dies and decays, where some babies survive and others don't. Here I could eat my sugary cereal and cry, wondering how I was going to protect us from harm in the future, knowing I couldn't.

A few weeks after my son got out of the hospital, our little family moved across the country, back home to Portland. We stayed with my parents for a few weeks while we waited for an apartment to open up in a complex I had my eye on. My mother had developed a penchant for collecting figures of Mary, a remnant of her Catholic girlhood shimmering through. She didn't want to worry or offend her Baptist friends, so she stored the collection of pictures and vases and figurines in the guest bedroom, the room I was staying in: the room where I still struggled with my fear and anxiety, clutching my tiny baby to me. I didn't want to leave that room, not ever. We had made it, we were safe, and I could never let anything bad happen to us again. For a few days everyone would check on us, worriedly. My husband, my mother, my father. But I mostly stayed in that room and nursed my baby, and I looked at all the images of Mary.

There was one picture in particular I couldn't take my eyes away from. Mary, looking sad, held a Jesus who was more toddler than baby. I looked at the picture and I understood: Mary knew her son was going to die from the beginning. And still, she loved him, and she loved the God who gave him to her as fiercely as any mother among us. Her life, her eyes, her work would be to live in the tension of those two places: always relinquishing her child, always holding him as close as she could for as long as possible. Mary, with her sad eyes, became my friend that day.

I stared at Mary as all of the prosperity gospels I had absorbed throughout the years began to crumble under the weight of reality. I thought of how easy it had been to believe that if only I did the right things and believed the right things and bought the right product and said the right prayers everything would turn out okay. In my mind, warped by the American obsession with safety and wellness and success, my failure—including suffering, sadness, anxiety, and sickness—had to be some sign that God was displeased with me.

There's a Joel Osteen sermon out there floating on the winds of social media. He's talking about how much God loves to give us good things, how God is a good Father. Osteen says that if his own children came up on the stage dressed in ragged clothes, we would rightly judge him to be a poor father, a terrible caregiver. People in the audience clap for this; God does not want his people to be poor or in need or sad or raggedy!

What would Osteen say to Mary? I wondered. Mary who was poor, maybe illiterate, young, destined to suffer and to give birth to someone who suffered. What would Osteen say about the rest of the Bible, chock full of stories of a God who was obsessed with people, especially the sad and unwell ones? Poverty or sickness or suffering, Jesus constantly pointed out, was not a sign of the absence of God's love or even a sign of sin. It was a sign of a broken world filled with people who exploited each other and created unjust systems that left a few wealthy and safe and well while the rest of society struggled to survive.

Prosperity gospels lurk within most of us, whether we see them or not. But as the Jesuit priest Father Greg Boyle says, God does not protect us from suffering, but God does promise to be with us in the suffering. Look at the beatitudes, that most glorious list of people that the American Dream would have us believe are to be pitied or perhaps are even on the wrong track with God: the poor, the sick, the sad, the meek, the oppressed. But Jesus says they are blessed—can I trust him when he says that?

It took me getting to the place where I was pretty poor, sick, and sad myself before this truly good news could start to seep into my bones. Locking myself in a spare bedroom to keep myself and my baby safe was a low point, but it exposed how deep the need for control is within me, how I long to believe anyone who promises the allures of safety and wellness for the people I love.

There, in that spare bedroom, I starting to build up a real faith from the bottom floor up. I was starting to believe maybe we humans did have a God with us, a God who, in this scenario, is the father and the mother and the child, a God who suffers and resurrects, giving us a hope that this could be true for us as well. In Mary I saw a mother who could model for me what it means to live with the work of God in mind. We cannot protect ourselves or our families, and this was never the point. But when we open ourselves up to the terror of love (because the underside of love is always grief) we will be joining in this endeavor with God, the one who is always being split wide open by joy and lament, children everywhere every day delighting God with their smiles and songs and creativity, breaking God's heart with their cruelty and selfishness, harrowing God's eyes with their sickness and accidents and catastrophes.

Pretty soon I got to the point where I could leave that bedroom, and eventually I too could join the land of the living, those who gathered the courage to keep going forward in a world of suffering, where safety and health and happy endings are never guaranteed. When I stole the picture of Mary from my mother's guest bedroom and hung it up in our new apartment, my mother didn't say a word. My mother knows. She knows how to keep on loving even after her world has ended, like so many mothers before her, including the mother of God.

16 ✶ THE SHIP OF THE DOOMED

On this mountain the Lord Almighty will prepare
a feast of rich food for all peoples. . . .
On this mountain he will destroy
the shroud that enfolds all peoples,
the sheet that covers all nations;
he will swallow up death forever.

ISAIAH 25:6-8 NIV

The second time I almost died in childbirth, I could not stop thinking about refugees.[1] Specifically, a boat full of Rohingya refugees who were seeking refuge and were not allowed to land anywhere—a ship of the doomed.[2] I heard about it in the feverish pitch of the hospital room where I was close to dying. Kept alive by machines and medicines, I caught snippets of the world outside of my bed with blurry eyes. My body had decided to fail. My tiny new baby needed me to get better faster than I was able.

At night, when I was the most alone, I thought about those people in the boat—the slow beeping of the monitors checking my blood pressure, my husband asleep in a chair, our baby in a plastic hospital crib. I could not reach my baby. Other people had to take care of the son I had fought so hard to bring into the world. I did not let myself feel sad about this. Instead, I thought about people who were suffering more. I thought about the boat people, the Rohingya. I saw their faces in my mind.

I had made it; my baby had been born. They had got me on the medicines before my heart burst. *We were lucky*, I told myself fiercely. The Christian language of my youth drifted up to the top of my mind. *We were a miracle.*

But were we? We had survived while little children starved to death on a boat that drifted from one closed country to another; the world watched silently as we all agreed there were some people too desperate to help. I turned over the faces of the people on the boat like rocks in my fingers. I wanted to make them smooth with my worry. I wanted to save them with my anguish. I, who had barely escaped death, wanted to save everyone else myself. I didn't trust God to do it anymore.

A few weeks after I left the hospital I had a dream. In the dream I sat at a long wooden table, which stretched into a black infinity. Not a terrifying blackness, a warm, electric darkness that spoke of saturation and richness. I was sitting in an oil painting, but with colors more real and more familiar. The props reminded me of the eighteenth and nineteenth centuries: wooden bowls full of artfully arranged fruit, rustic loaves of bread scattered in the middle. I was on a bench at the longest table of my life, quietly and with my hands folded in my lap. Around me people were eating and laughing and talking with each other—people I somehow both knew and did not know, people I recognized but had never met. They were throwing a party to which I had somehow snagged an invitation. I squinted at their faces—men, women, and children, and suddenly I knew where I had seen them. I had seen these faces on CNN. Dark brown skin, black hair, lines of worry worn into the creases around their eyes. These friends, all around me, were the Rohingya refugees who fled their country and got on a boat, desperate to escape those who wanted them eradicated. I watched them, joy radiating from their faces, and then I picked up a piece of bread to eat along with them. I heard an audible voice so loud it woke me. This is what heaven is like. I heard a voice full of timbre, both inside and outside my experience. "In heaven, you will feast with those who have suffered the most on earth."

I woke up with a heavy blanket of peace around me for the first time in months. I luxuriated in that feeling, willing it to never leave. But of course it did. When I turned on the news again, there was always another story of suffering, another story of people in need, and a world which was bound and determined to look away.

★ ★ ★

My friend Jessica has lived and worked with refugees in the city of Austin, Texas. Recently she wrote a book called *After the Last Border*, detailing the experiences of two women who had resettled in the United States from very different backgrounds. In writing her book my friend became deeply imbedded in the history of the US Refugee Resettlement program. She focused on a particular moment, one that most Americans have forgotten. In 1939 there was a ship filled with almost a thousand Jewish refugees who had fled the terrible night known as Kristallnacht, when the German army razed synagogues, killed Jewish citizens, and started sending people to concentration camps.

The few who could got on large boats and tried to flee to safety. First Cuba, and then the United States ultimately denied them access or entry, even going so far as to have ships with guns stationed in case people tried to swim to shore. The people who had fled Germany for their lives and the lives of their children could see the land, the promise of safety. But the United States said no; better safe than sorry is what then-president Roosevelt decided.

It's estimated that over half of those refugees—for that is what they were, before there was a legal term for it—ended up in concentration camps. Sent back to the hell that they had tried to escape, so close to freedom, yet sailing on a ship of the doomed, a ship deemed unsafe.[3]

Of course we would have reacted differently, wouldn't we? If people in the United States had known the extent of Hitler's schemes, wouldn't we have welcomed in the boats of the desperate? Current events tell us otherwise. The narrative continues on a loop: desperate families seeking shelter, twisted by politics and popular imagination into the violent, the unsafe. They will take our jobs or kill our children; they are strangers, not neighbors. We have no responsibility to them.

As a child growing up I remember learning about the Holocaust in the hushed tones of the still shocked. Wasn't it unbelievable? That educated, Westernized, advanced, Christian White men and women could do such a thing? There was a horror underlying my education in this regard that seems misplaced now. It is believable because it happened. And part of the reason why so many were killed, why so many were tortured, was because the people who could have given them shelter shut their doors and minds and hearts to their neighbors in need.

The story goes that after all of the evidence of the Jewish genocide came to light, the US Refugee Resettlement program was born out of the ashes of WWII and the atrocities it highlighted. Thanks to the tireless work of survivors and others, a government program to help resettle people who would otherwise perish became a moral imperative.

★ ★ ★

In the beginning the refugee resettlement program primarily focused on English-speaking, educated, professionals from war-torn countries. In recent decades, however, as conflicts continue to grow and as our world enters a time of mass displacement unlike any we have ever seen, the program has focused on human rights abuses, seeking to resettle people who have experienced the most discrimination or been allies of some sort in conflicts where the United States has been involved. This is why we saw waves of Hmong refugees, then Sudanese (including the lost boys), then Somali and Somali Bantu, then Afghan and Syrian refugees.

I did not know these roots—in fact I knew little at all—when I first started volunteering with refugees in my own city of Portland more than fifteen years ago. These families from half a world away were simply miracles, and I accepted them as such. Later, a few questions would surface. Why this family and not another? Who gets chosen, and what is the reasoning? Deep into both the refugee crisis and our country's response to it, I engaged with new-to-me neighbors who had survived the very worst the world has to offer. I got a degree in teaching English to speakers of others languages, and I tried to focus specifically on literacy. Many of the women I met and worked with and lived with and taught had never been to school. The common denominator, the thing all of them had in common, was some kind of trauma—the trauma of poverty or of being female in a patriarchal society or the disruption of education due to war or famine or an oppressive government regime. The people I met were survivors. They were the lucky few, the less than 1 percent of refugees that get resettled worldwide.

* * *

I think I might have a touch of secondary trauma. I never ask for stories, I have never sat down and asked a friend or neighbor who has experienced forced migration to tell me the horrors they have outrun. But sometimes the stories just pour out. There is the woman who scrubbed her daughter's face of bright red cherry juice while she told me how all the female engineers like herself were killed or driven out of her old city. There is the friend who works herself to the bone going to community college and taking care of her four children, who politely interrupts me when I beg her to take a break. "Whenever my mother calls me from our country, the first thing she asks is if I am going to school. Because when I was eighth grade the Taliban came, and I wasn't allowed to go to school anymore."

There are the women who tell me their family was wonderful, not too poor, that some of their sisters got to go to school even. But they themselves were the ones who had to stay and watch the goats or get married at age fourteen or watch the children of their brothers. The women in my English classes who tell the stories of their families, both the children that survived and the children they have buried. And most of them have at least one, if not multiple, sad stories to tell.

A few years ago, when my daughter was seven and my son almost two, I found myself in an elementary school cafeteria that smelled faintly of boiled vegetables. The room was windowless, the linoleum was swept clean and furnished with picnic-style tables pushed next to each other to create long rows. My toddler and I were desperate for friends, and so once a week I would dust off my English teaching degree and break out my materials. I went to the weekly class with ginger-molasses cookies. I made coffee as the women showed up. I printed worksheets full of phrases I hoped might make their lives the tiniest bit easier. I tried to communicate love in small ways in this weekly ritual of practicing English in our elementary school cafeteria. My neighbors came to my class, shy at first, then smiling broadly, their shyness effaced by the presence of a blond-haired toddler. They touched my son's face. They stroked his hair. They took pictures and sent them to distant family members.

One morning I settled in at a cafeteria table with three new women, all of them bright-eyed, wearing colorful headscarves. They breezed through my assessment questions: they knew the alphabet and could tell me their addresses. I asked them how long they had lived in my city and what language they spoke and where they were from. The leader (there is always a leader) answered for everyone. She was older than the other two. She wore lilac polyester pants, a flower-printed hijab, a shirt with sequins surrounding the sleeves, a hint of lipstick on her bright face. This woman told me that had all come to Portland in the past year, that they speak Rohingya, and that they are from Myanmar.

I asked her to repeat herself, and she said it again. "You, you speak Rohingya?" I asked, peering closer at her face. "Yes," she said. "Yes, I speak Rohingya. I *am* Rohingya." The other women sitting at the table beamed at me and nod. Yes, they are Rohingya too. I surprised them with the force of my enthusiasm. "Rohingya!" I nearly shrieked. "Here, in Portland!"

They drank the coffee I poured into Styrofoam cups, too much sugar and powdered creamer for my taste, perfect for theirs. They ate the cookies I made and brought out a tin of almond biscuits to share. They tried to make my son laugh, but he refused. He whined at me until the oldest woman gave him a cookie, forever buying his stubborn love.

They are the lucky ones, the ones whose ships or airplanes made it here. Our limited shared language failed us, and the trails that brought them to my school cafeteria remain inscrutable, mysterious. They were simply there, at that moment, sitting with me. They were some of the last refugees to make it into my city before policies started changing. Before the US refugee resettlement was slowly dismantled, piece by piece, in front of our eyes. But at that moment, we didn't know. We simply ate cookies and drank chai together, experiencing the tiniest taste of how big God's dream for the world is. How God sees every ship of the doomed, every stateless wanderer, and every lonely girl longing to do good.

I thought back to the dream I had when I had almost died. And I thought about the day it was redeemed, where I sat at a long table together with those who have suffered so much on earth, acutely aware of the love of God for them and myself at that moment. We sat at a table in an easy silence born of a desire to stretch that moment as long as possible. When the class was over, I pushed my son's stroller home, and the women walked back with me. I waved at them from my front stoop as they continued to their own apartments. I will see them, nearly every day, walking to and from school together, gathering our children and taking them home. Every Friday we will feast together in the house of joy known as one of the lowest-rated schools in the state. We will drink our coffee and eat our cookies. We will sit in the mystery of being alive, of what it means to be a miracle in a world of suffering, for that one hour every week.

17 ✶ GOOD SEEDS

I WAS AT A MISSIONS CONFERENCE about a decade ago, sitting next to my parents in the front row of a megachurch. I was excited to be surrounded by people who were talking about overseas work and unreached people groups. I loved being in a large auditorium filled with flags from countries all over the world and missionaries wearing the traditional dress of whatever country they served in. Growing up I had prayed for a specific calling, a specific country or people group to be placed on my heart. In college I sat in chapels waiting desperately for my chance to go and be of use to God and the world.

So there I was again. The familiarity of the subject was soothing to me. I practically had Matthew 28:19 tattooed into my brain: "Go into all the world and make disciples from all the nations."[1] I was comfortable in these spaces, where we were all on the same page, the spiritually elite and the culturally backward. I sat in the front of the auditorium because I cared so much. I wanted to be so close to all the action.

The man who was speaking that night was a famous apologist, someone who wrote best-selling books about Christianity. I don't remember much of what he said that night, but I do remember a video he shared. On a widescreen he showed a packed house a video detailing how Islam was taking over Europe. The video had foreboding music and terrible graphics showing how Muslims had so many children (brown figures multiplying) while Europeans had declining birth rates (white figures shrinking ever smaller). In the coming decades, the narrator intoned in an ominous voice, there would be more mosques than churches in Europe. The message implied was one of doom and terror, of civilization being over. The film was eight minutes long, and my stomach tightened more and more as the predictions got worse and worse. At the very end, in a faster and quieter voice, the narrator told us, the audience, to go out and preach the good news to Muslims. The house lights went back on, and the famous man began to talk again.

But I couldn't listen. I stared up at the speaker as he spoke, lit up by hot lights on the stage. He was actively trying to make people afraid of Islam and Muslims. He had given us no information in the video other than birth rates. It seemed a strange point to focus on, and I wondered what it had to do with the gospel. Was this truly a video asking us to love Muslims and preach the good news? Or was it thinly veiled anxiety about losing power? The questions were sown in my heart that evening and continued to bloom in the next few decades. The proof, I decided, would be in the fruit of all of us attending these conferences, eager to spread the good news. You can't love somebody if you are determined to be afraid of them. Perhaps that's why the Bible is full of the messengers of God telling everyone to "fear not." It is our human impulse to fear. And it is our human impulse to baptize it under religious language.

I left that missions conference with a heaviness I did not want to articulate. For years I took classes, read books, did extracurricular courses, attended conferences; I learned from people who said they wanted to love "the unreached." But oftentimes there was a current of supremacy and even fear lacing these discussions. I was starting to realize that many people believed we should focus on Muslim ministry not because they were valuable people made in the image of God but because they posed the biggest threat. The question remained unanswered: the biggest threat to what, exactly?

★ ★ ★

I have many friends who have worked at refugee resettlement agencies. Since 2016 the change has been acute, due in part to changing attitudes but mostly due to changing policies. For the past few years the United States has reached historic lows in the number of refugees we will allow to be resettled—18,000 for 2020 when the average has consistently been closer to 75,000 (President Reagan himself set the average around 89,000).[2] As I write this, President Trump is being advised to lower the number of refugees admitted to the United States to none, a process called "zeroing out." The trickle-down effects of simply denying vulnerable people one of the few pathways to citizenship in our country are large: as quotas are lowered (and not even fulfilled), as fewer visas are given out, resettlement agencies lose their funding because they aren't doing their jobs in the eyes of the government. Resettlement agencies, including evangelical organizations like World Relief, have had to shutter dozens of offices and lay off employees (including caseworkers who are formerly resettled refugees themselves).

Even if, by a miracle, the gates were suddenly opened again to the desperate of the world, there would be no way to receive them because there are so few people left to do the work of resettlement. By conservative estimates by those who work in these fields such as Matthew Soerens and Jenny Yang of World Relief, it will take decades for the program to get back to the place it was in the last few years of the Obama administration or even to the previous average of 75,000 a year.[3]

As someone who teaches English to recently arrived refugees, I can see for myself how the very landscape of my life, my country, and my neighborhood has already changed. New people are no longer coming because policies have been implemented and effectively shut the already narrow doors—as I write this, I haven't had a new English for Speakers of Other Languages student in almost two years. While the global refugee crisis continues to grow around the world, the fears of our age have solidified into actual policies that devastate actual lives. And the only way to change it is to fix it the same way. To change hearts and minds, to expand our idea of who our neighbors are and what our responsibility is to them, and to then change the policies themselves.

★ ★ ★

I don't remember how I met my friend Aisha, but I remember I was immediately drawn to her. She wore a headscarf, tiny wire-rimmed glasses, and a large smile. Her English was gorgeous, characterized by an accent I couldn't quite place. Our children were in the same first-grade class at school. She lived in apartments across the train tracks, and when I invited her to come to my younger son's birthday party at my house, she came with her three children in tow. Her youngest was the same age as my son, who was turning two that day. Her son, whose name means "peace," was slightly sick. Glassy-eyed, he didn't move from his mother's lap, silent and staring at the festivities around him.

My mother, a self-described "professional grandmother," went up to Aisha and gently asked if she could hold the boy. Aisha nodded her head, and my mother sat in a chair on my back deck for what seemed like hours, gently swaying with a sick little boy, occasionally giving him sips of juice. A few weeks later, Aisha came up to me at school. She pulled me aside in the corner of the cafeteria because she wanted to tell me something. She wanted to talk about my mom. She told me that she had lived in the United Stated for three years and that her youngest son had been born here. But she was so isolated: there was no one from her family here, no one from her clan in Portland, no one was even there to cook her the traditional soup served to a woman who has a new baby. No one from her home country was near to look after her once she gave birth to her son. She lived so far from her mother and her brothers and sisters, she told me.

"Your mother," Aisha told me, "your mother held my son at the party. And I cried because that is the first time someone besides me or my husband have held that child for these two years." She started crying as she told me this, and so did I. I cried thinking about the beauty of my mom instinctively reaching out for a child who'd never known his own grandmother's touch, of swaying and comforting a child as any good grandmother would. But I also cried for the sadness of it all, to think of the years of isolation, of needing help and having none, for the fact that Aisha was so well-acquainted with such profound isolation. My mother now visits Aisha regularly. She is an adopted grandmother, not only to Aisha's son but to several other families in my neighborhood.

There is no way we can move forward in welcoming the stranger in the United States if we don't assess the situation honestly: our morality has slipped to the point where we do not care that people will suffer and die due to our own desire for safety. In fact, according to polls put out by Pew Research, White evangelicals were the least likely group to identify a moral need to resettle refugees (with only 25 percent saying we should).

The value of safety in an age of fear has been twisted to the point that people who read the Bible (with its myriad references to welcoming, loving, and supporting justice for the stranger in their midst) can feel no obligation toward the actual foreigner in dire need of help. And this has real consequences. Aisha cannot see her mother or brothers or sisters because they live in a country where it is not safe for her husband to go back to, and she lives in a country where her family is currently banned from entry. She lives in the tension that most of my neighbors live in: gratitude and sorrow mingled together. A wish for another world, one where they could be safe and still in their country, their culture, with their family.

From an early age I puzzled over a question I wonder if everyone has asked themselves: if the tables were turned—if we had been born on the other side of the world, into a different family, religion, race, economic situation—what would we want? People in positions of safety and privilege must learn to grapple with how they use what they've been given: as a welcome mat or as a shield?

★ ★ ★

Aisha made it to safety, just barely. She had to flee her town when it was set on fire, when people targeted her city due to their ethnicity. She has one badly damaged book of photographs, pictures from her wedding where she should look gorgeous, radiant, full of possibility. But instead the photos are warped almost beyond recognition. Still, she shows it to me one day because it is all she has. The day she shows it to me is a day that Donald Trump is holding a press conference about the need to build a larger wall on the US-Mexican border. I think about walls as metaphors, how the problem isn't the concrete or the steel being used to secure a border but the reasoning behind it. Everyone wants to be safe, both the people who voted for the wall and people like Aisha. Who should we listen to the most? Who is truly in danger?

I think of Aisha and her son. Her son, born in a new land, one where her mother cannot visit. And yet she gave him a name that means "peace" as an act of defiance. Do we really want safety? Or do we want true peace? As Aisha and countless prophets and poets in the Scriptures will tell us, there is no way to guarantee safety in the world. The only way to move forward is with righteousness—true justice and equality for all. Then, and only then, will we ever experience a measure of peace that will ripple forth into the next generations, reminding them that they once were the ones in need and could be again someday.

A few years ago my mother pulled me aside to tell me something herself. Even though she had met many refugees through me throughout the years—visiting my English classes, saying hello to neighbors—she still had been afraid of Muslims. She was surrounded by people who listened to news and commentators that constantly told her how dangerous they are, so this fear had been planted and sustained for many years. She attended the missions conferences that I had and absorbed the belief that our culture was at war with theirs. I was taken aback. My mother had met my friends, had smiled at them and seemed fine, and all the while she was harboring this fear.

What changed, I asked her? It was becoming family, she said. It was entering into their lives and seeing their reality: as women who wanted to follow God, who loved their families, who had lived through hell, who were determined to move forth in the world with joy and resilience. It was recognizing the need for family bonds to be built. My mother, like me, fell in love with our Muslim friends primarily because they appealed to our very religious hearts. In their communities we found people who loved and wanted to be obedient to God. The

Muslims I met embodied many of the characteristics I was raised to value as an evangelical; I was constantly surprised to discover that we had so much in common.

My mother now stands up in her church and tells anyone who will listen about the blessing of Muslim refugees, how they have strengthened her faith in God, how they cook for her and share their families with her, how her life has opened up in new and mysterious and miraculous ways. Most people nod their heads and perhaps even wipe their eyes, but much of the fear remains. Decades of conditioning cannot easily be undone by one story or by one encounter.

I think about my own two children, how they beg to visit the apartments of our Muslim neighbors. They love visiting because they know they will be adored. Our Muslim friends think that children are a blessing from God and treat them accordingly. They do not have multiple children in some nefarious plot to take over the world. Their religion and relationship to God influence these decisions—who are they to deny these good gifts God gives—similar to Catholic theology. For years my neighbors have stuffed my children full of cookies and candy bars, have shown up to our birthday parties with gaudy electronic cars, have pestered me mercilessly to have six more children. Their love and joy in children and family relationships is palpable and often countercultural to my American peers.

My children feel safe in spaces with Muslim neighbors; they feel seen and known and valued, more than they do in most other places. My greatest hope for my children remains ever the same: that they would grow up rooted in the love of Christ, that they are known and valued and loved. They get some of this knowledge from interacting with our neighbors and the belovedness that is heaped on them with every sugary treat or plate piled high with rice. But I also pray that they would have eyes to see how successful fear is at twisting narratives for specific purposes. I want them to focus not so much on going out into the world and making disciples, but flipping the narrative on its head: to joyfully welcome the world as it shifts and moves ever forward, bringing into our cities and neighborhoods and homes the chance to be discipled together as a community, as a global family, into the ways of Jesus.

18 ★ WAKING UP SAD

Once I was in a writing workshop with a beautiful, strong woman. She pulled me aside the last day of the week and stood close to me. She told me that she maybe had a word from God for me. I had heard this often enough in my youth, I tried to make my face smooth and judgment free, but my shoulders tensed. The woman looked at me intently, and I tried to look back without wavering. What if, she said to me, as solemn as a prophet—what if you woke up one morning and were . . . happy? She let that sentence hang in the air for a moment, letting me understand the full impact. How would that change your life? How would that change your writing? What would happen to you if you woke up one morning and—poof!—you were no longer angry at the world?

I didn't have a good response other than to feel the shame spread out in my throat. But I nodded my head and murmured something about how she was right; I should try to be more pleasant. But in my mind I was remembering a friend who talked often about soldiers and PTSD. "They're the ones with the normal response," he once said. "It's the ones who say absolutely nothing is wrong who we should be worried about."

This woman told me she wanted to have a prayer time for me before the week was out. I nodded my head again, but every time I saw her I managed to slip out of her path unnoticed. I did not want her beautiful hand pressing on my shoulder, I did not want her praying to God to bless me with happiness. Instead, more than anything, I wanted her—this talented, driven, complicated woman—to wake up sad herself.

★ ★ ★

One day a teacher at my daughter's school pulled me aside and said, "If you know any parents who are undocumented, tell them to have a plan in place for their kids." I stared at her. She was looking at the children streaming out of the classrooms, moving like a great tide toward the exit doors. She talked to me while keeping her eyes on them, a walkie-talkie on her hip. "Tell everyone you know that they need to have family members or neighbors or friends—someone, anyone—who can step in and take care of the kids if they are deported." I looked at her, both astonished and empty. "I don't know that many people," I said, and I can't believe we are truly having this conversation.

She told me, "I was in Arizona when the SB 1070 laws went down. Kids would go home from school to empty houses, both parents gone, deported. I know it happens. We have to be prepared that it could happen here." I nodded and collected my daughter, glancing at the parents I normally smiled at. I walked home, looking at my daughter's blonde head surrounded by a sea of black and brown. Kids ran into the street, and I yelled at them to stay to the side. Boys threw pebbles into the puddles, they took off their backpacks and flung them at each other. Children ran back to their houses and their apartments; they disappeared inside doors into circumstances that to me are blurry, a fog of unknowing.

A few months ago, when Donald Trump was elected president of the United States, one of the mothers at school told me her son was worried. He kept coming to her, crying, saying "Mom, Mom, what will I do if you get deported?" She is a single mother, and she works at a fast food restaurant nearby. She comes one morning a week to volunteer at the school. "Who is telling him this?" she wants to know. "Is it the teachers?" "No," I reply. "I think it's just that all of the kids are talking about it, all the time." She tells me what she told her son: that yes, Donald Trump is the president now, but he has many more important things to worry about then deporting her. She tells her son to stop worrying, that they have to have hope for the future, that they cannot live in fear. Her voice is calm and she smiles reassuringly, and I go back home feeling slightly better.

But later I thought about this conversation. This mother never told her son that it wouldn't happen, that she wouldn't be forced to leave. She is not a mother who lies or who makes false promises. I think about this mother, how she is trying to help start a PTA at our school, how she is always smiling at me, how she sits in the cafeteria with her son in the mornings while he eats breakfast. I know I am supposed to focus on her resilience, be inspired by her words in regards to not living in fear. But instead I lie awake at night and imagine a heat map of my neighborhood, the ugly little ranch homes and the large apartment complexes, the red showing up as fear. I imagine all the worried little children, the boys and girls who know what it is to anticipate the end of life as they know it. My heart is a sponge, and I am soaking up all that worry and fear and stress, tossing and turning until morning.

* * *

Once, I was on a train to Seattle. I was desperately excited about the chance to go to a writing retreat on an island. I was escaping all that tugged at my eyes and my brain—my children, my neighbors, the news of my country and its policies that punished everyone I held dear. I sat on a train and dreamily looked out the window. My seatmate, a man close to my age with tattoos covering his arms and creeping up his neck, took out a black bandana and put it over his eyes. He slept, quietly, while I wrote in my journal. Messy, unintelligible writing, my hand trying to keep up with my thoughts.

As I was writing in my journal, the train stopped. The voice overhead sad, "There will be an hour delay. There has been a trespassing incident." Passengers got up and stretched. I checked the time, worried that I might miss my ride to the ferry that would take me to the island. My seatmate woke up. The party behind us, who sounded as though they were drinking even though it was only 10 in the morning, played their card games and complained about the delay. Finally, we started moving again, the slow scenery changing from beautiful to mundane to run-down, over and over again. Fields and forest, homeless camps erected in the shadow of industry, small towns with a few stoplights.

As we rolled through one such town, I noticed large black SUVs, yellow caution tape, police officers standing together in clumps. A woman standing in the middle of the tracks parallel to the ones we were on, an entire train station closed. As we slowly sailed by, I saw the woman wearing gloves clutching a semiopaque plastic bag. The bag was filled with something heavy, something wet. I started to see streaks of dark brown, of red, on the sides of the platform. I saw a torso, on the tracks. A few meters down, a leg. I gasped so loudly it startled the man next to me. "Don't look," I told him, covering my face in my hands. But he did, standing up in his seat and leaning over me. Other people started to murmur, craning their necks, "Oh my god, what was that?"

Minutes went by in silence. Then my seatmate shifted in his seat toward me. He exhaled loudly and asked if I was okay. I said yes because I didn't know what else to say. He started talking, and he didn't stop until we got to Seattle. It was the anniversary of his best friend's death, and he was shaken up. He had a bad relationship with his dad. Life was incredibly fragile, and we had to treat it like a gift, you know? He was clean and sober these days. Working a good restaurant job now. He couldn't believe what he had just caught a glimpse of. He took this train constantly, and this sort of thing never happened.

In my mind I willed myself to listen. How would a pastor respond? They would comfort, they would offer assurances, they would fill in the gaps of meaning-making. *A good person would do this*, I thought to myself. But deep down I knew I wasn't a good person. I wanted my seatmate to stop talking to me, to stop needing me to assure him it would all be fine. I instead wanted to think about what I had seen on the tracks. I wanted to find out who it was. In my mind I crafted a narrative about a man, older and with no house and no loved ones, who saw a train coming and walked purposefully in front of it.

I nodded my head as my seatmate talked and talked and talked. The rest of the week on the island I tried to pretend that I was fine. But I couldn't write that entire week long, surrounded by gorgeous old-growth forests and rocky Pacific Northwest beaches. I googled what happened at that tiny train station, and the police report confirmed I was right. I reread my journal, where I had been writing just before I witnessed the violence of a public suicide, the ending of a very sad story. I had been writing, just at that moment, this: "I am so tired of noticing," I wrote. "I am so tired of not being able to shut everything down. If this is a gift from God, it often feels like a curse."

Professor Yolanda Norton talks about how Jesus lives into the role of the prophet as laid out in the Hebrew Scriptures. Norton reveals that biblical prophets are local, they have a divine imperative to critique the powers that be, they work to energize the people, and they live in anguish with the people. For Norton all of these characteristics together are important. A prophet doesn't just critique without energizing the people with an alternative vision for the future. The prophet doesn't live in a state of perpetual anger but instead lives into anguish and lament with the people.

I am generally skeptical of those who call themselves prophets. But I do believe more of us ought to reclaim the role of someone who critiques the powers of the world and sits in the anguish of the broken world. Someone who refuses to capitulate to despair and instead sees hope in a new vision for the world couched in the goodness of a God who restores. Professor Norton once told a group of us gathered for a conference that one of the words for prophet in Hebrew is *nabi*, which means "someone who causes things to bubble up." This definition strikes me as profoundly important. Not the loudest voice in the room, not the one screaming about problems or coming up with quick and easy solutions that cost people little and change nothing about power. Instead, a prophet is someone who helps ensure that the truth comes to light, that what is hidden in the depths of our hearts and in our social, political, economic, and theological systems comes to the surface for us to actually deal with.

Within the prophetic works of Scripture I find contradictions and proclamations that soothe my mind. I see people who tell the truth, point out injustice, grieve for the world, and hope in a better future, a future where people do not crush each other for profit but work together for flourishing. In the poets and the prophets of old I see the same desire: we cannot rest until the whole world is right. And in the meantime we will alternately fast and feast, we will be faithful to the festivals and the laments. I am okay with being sad much of the time. And yet I also recognize that a hallmark of empire is how it prefers that people operate in a constant state of despair. Depressed people are easier to control. People lose their will to fight. The imagination to believe another world is possible falls through their fingers like sand.

In the work of paying attention I can sometimes be overwhelmed by injustice. It is so systemic, so pervasive, and I have largely benefited from it. There is no easy resolution to this, and grief and lament and truth-telling are necessary components for how to move forward in a world that would prefer us to accept the status quo.

I can't make myself wake up happy, as much as I have tried. Nor do I see it as a value worth pursuing. But despair, or sadness, doesn't help anyone. In fact, it can be another form of self-absorption, the flip side of a savior complex—the failure complex. This is why it's important to reclaim the discipline of lament. Lament in the Bible is not just an airing of grievances, pointing out what is sad and horrible in the world while the people in power insist all is well (although that is a part of it). It is a sign of radical hope in a God who is listening. It is people feeling close enough to God to pour forth what is in their hearts and people trusting God enough to believe that another world might be possible.

Walter Brueggemann talks about the prophet Jeremiah's ministry of articulated grief. Part of Jeremiah's ministry was simply to be a witness to the unbelief and destruction of his people, to name the unnamed. Why is this so powerful, the call to describe exactly how terrible reality is? Brueggemann posits it is because we live in a world where there is the ever-present danger of what he called "the royal consciousness"—the voices of the powerful telling us that everything is fine when it is not.

Scrolling through Instagram I see post after post of people happy, wealthy, and successful. Their kids are in perfect schools, their health is fixed by essential oils, their theologies are so neat and sure and fit in a loopy font overlaid over majestic mountains. It is not the fault of the people posting those pictures, exactly. We have all been trained to carefully curate our lives for various reasons. But still, their happiness for all to see on display wounds me. In it I see the threads of forgetfulness, of our human tendency to forget our responsibility to one another and of wanting to keep it that way.

★ ★ ★

Once I saw a self-care expert on Instagram asking people to think about what it would take for them to be happy. I asked myself that question and was shocked at how quickly the answer popped into my head: I will never be happy until every single person in the world is safe, happy, and flourishing. I was both pleased and miserable at my core longing. I was pleased because it spoke to a spark of the divine in me because I do believe that this is God's dream for the world. I think this is what shalom is, what the kingdom of God makes possible. But I was also miserable because until the kingdom comes in full, until we are in the new creation, this isn't a reality. There will always be suffering, so how am I to live in the meantime? I cannot choose, I cannot blandly accept the cruelties of the world, nor can I save it with my outsider tears. I do what I've always done: I will hurtle through life, ricocheting between misery and delight, between sorrow and joy. I will be a cup filled to the brim with despair and hope, constantly spilling onto everyone around me.

Sometimes in order to accept something for ourselves, we need to see it through a different lens. I am perhaps fine with accepting that I will always wake up sad. But what if I asked it in another way? Do I want my neighbors to wake up sad? Do I want my own children to grow up with happiness as the main value of their lives? It's an interesting question, one that reframes my mind. I do desperately wish for my daughter to learn to love her neighbors, especially the neighbors God was and is obsessed with: the poor, the oppressed, the vulnerable. But deeper than this wish is something more primal, a desire for my daughter to know she is loved.

What good is anything else she can do in the world if inside of her heart she feels a lack, if she is trying to prove something, if she is trying to save the world herself or atone for her own sins or bully people into needing her? If she doesn't grow up feeling loved by God, then the rest of her life will be oriented around extracting and exploiting that love from others.

I feel a great heavy weight of duty coupled with the joy of living with my neighbors in mind. I will never wake up to a neighborhood where every soul in every house and apartment is at peace. I will never see true shalom in my life, which hollows out a part of my soul. But do I have the eyes to see the tiniest flashes of shalom? The glimpses that make me believe another world is possible—that even now it is coming and will be brought by a God who loves and sees and delights more than I can ever understand? I wake up sad, I kiss the cheeks of my children, and I drink the coffee my husband makes for me every morning. I savor the coffee as long as I can, stretching out the simplest pleasures before me. I cannot save the whole world, I cannot heal it with my own two hands. But I can live in it, I can speak the truth about where it is broken, and where it is being repaired. I can gather the courage from my friends who have experienced exile, and I can try to imitate them as best as I can. I can try to be brave enough to keep noticing, even when it breaks my heart at every turn.

19 ★ THE HAPPIEST PLACE ON EARTH

A FEW YEARS AGO MY HUSBAND AND I went to Disneyland to celebrate our ten-year anniversary. I'm not someone you'd think would love Disneyland. I pride myself on rejecting artifice, on embracing authenticity; I'm obsessed with inequality and poverty; I lie awake at night trying to solve the problems of the world. But once I am in Disneyland, I lose my mind just a little bit. There's so much magic, such well-manicured trees, spotless buildings, and visually entrancing rides, variations on classic songs I've heard since I was a child piped in around every corner, a sort of nostalgic light show happening in my brain, bursting forth with warmth and pleasure. I can finally be carefree because millions of dollars have been poured into helping me forget that another world exists outside of this magic kingdom.

I spent much of my time in the section of Disneyland known Fantasyland, eating hot churros and ruminating on the cartoons I grew up watching. All the old Disney films were morality tales, in a way, designed to tell children how to act in a society that craved order. The original stories—modeled on old storytelling traditions like the Brothers Grimm—warned children to be obedient to their parents or they would die horrible deaths. I thought about this as I waited in line, surrounded by children melting down due to overstimulation. I daydreamed about which classic Christian vices correlated to which early Disney film. Mr. Toad was gluttony. Pinocchio was lust. Peter Pan was avarice or greed. Snow White's stepmother was envy, and so on and so forth. I wandered the rides in the park built for small children, stretching to make moralistic connections wherever I could.

By the end of the day my nose was sunburned, my feet ached, and I felt weary but good. As we left the park, driving back toward our budget hotel, I saw something: a group of protestors holding up signs.

"We Are the Dreamers, Save DACA," the signs said. I only caught a flash of them before we were past. I looked them up later, and yes—there was a small protest staged at Disneyland that day to ask the US government to save the DACA program, which gave undocumented youths a legal pathway to go to college and work. The program had been in flux since the 2016 election, leaving millions vulnerable and scared and no path forward. The slogans affixed to pieces of wood and held up high in the air were literal signs for me that pierced through the sparkling bubble I'd been surrounded by all day.

There is a world of fairy tales, of the stories we tell and retell our children, and there is also the world of suffering. Perhaps they are more closely linked than we would like to believe. How can we start to live into this tension instead of ricocheting back and forth between fantasy and despair, the cycle of burnout and self-care?

* * *

I'm fascinated by the ethical tangles involved in taking vacations or indulgence or treating myself. On my ten-year anniversary I was forced to ask myself some hard questions: Is going to Disneyland my form of self-care? Is it something I "earned" by my hard work, by making money, by being overwhelmed with the world? Is it a place to celebrate, to enjoy time with my husband, to engage in nostalgia and let my inner child (who is only slightly less judgmental than my actual self) run free? Perhaps it's all of that, and something more. I've learned that we don't always understand our minds or the ways they work, but our desires can point to deeper longings.

Self-care is a concept I hear bandied about constantly, especially from privileged people. But often the conversation centers on consumerism (try this bubble bath or this glass of rosé and everything will be fine!) and never gets to the actual itch begging to be scratched. But I've also heard people wondering about how to best care for ourselves and others in a way that's couched in an awareness of the realities of the world. How do we cope with things not being right, when we are exposed to the underbelly of the American dream? When we enter into relationship with people who have or who are suffering, and there's no easy fix? What do we do when we start to despair, when our light starts to dim?

Learning from nondominant cultures is crucial to understanding our longings for self-care as really being deeper desires for true peace. As Audre Lorde, a prominent African American poet and activist, once wrote, "Caring for myself is not self-indulgence; it is self-preservation, and that is an act of political warfare." Lorde did seek out avenues of self-care, but her goal was not to be cozy. Rather, her goal was surviving, thriving, and working toward justice. Writer Jamila Reddy, reflecting on Lorde's words, takes it a step further by pointing out that taking care of oneself—by making doctor's appointments, for example—will not always feel good. Self-care, she writes, "means I have to let myself grieve even though it hurts, or admit that I'm really not okay when I'd rather nobody know."[1] In other words, it involves the deeper work of inward character building and outward community building. It requires what Eugene Peterson calls "a long obedience in the same direction."[2] And it entails resilience, the long work of showing up, day in and day out, to see God's kingdom come on earth as it is in heaven.

★ ★ ★

Disneyland as a place of resilience building is a little far-fetched. And yet I am learning to pay attention to both the pleasure I found being immersed in the fantastical stories of my youth and the discord I felt when faced with the reality of the DACA protestors. I sometimes long to escape to a fantasy world where the good girl always wins and the bad villain is always punished; meanwhile, there are children who have grown up in my country who dream of being afforded basic citizenship privileges like the ability to work or go to college. What dreamers are we listening to?

The day after we went to Disneyland, we drove to another part of Los Angeles, a part that was surrounded by historical museums as well as the oldest street market in the city. We entered a nondescript corner building called Homeboy Industries, site of the largest gang-intervention and rehabilitation program in the United States. It's a place made famous by Father Greg Boyle, a Jesuit priest who started the program several decades ago. My husband and I toured the facilities, chatted with our guide (a former gang member) about his experiences, and ended by buying one of the best cinnamon rolls I have ever eaten in my life, lovingly handed to us by a man with tattoos running up and down his face. It was a few hours spent in another world—a world where both devastating things happen (gun violence, abuse, parental neglect, systematic oppression) and also miracles are expected and celebrated constantly. There were classes on trauma, parenting, yoga, and creative writing. There was a bakery and restaurant, a print shop, and a tattoo removal ministry. There was a culture of care and humor and a recognition of who the experts were in the space: the people who continued to practice resurrection, every day, believing themselves to be loved by God—the truly radical belief that can change our world.

Outside Homeboy Industries there's a word spray-painted next to a pair of angel wings. It's the word that Father Boyle is obsessed with: *kinship*. Father Boyle is not a fan of self-care; he, like many others, sees burnout coming from a position of the savior complex. When we engage in helping or serving people from a position of hierarchy, where we take on the tasks best left for God, we can become overwhelmed. But kinship—being intimately connected with another person—changes the equation. Father Boyle's aim in life is to seek a compassion that stands in awe at what people have to carry rather than in judgment at how they carry it. Father Boyle engages in regular rhythms and routines of resilience: prayer, retreats, resting when he needs to, but relationships based on compassion, mutuality, and awe don't lead to burnout. Instead, they are the building blocks of a life where delight is just as likely to surprise you as suffering.

Lisa Sharon Harper, author of *The Very Good Gospel*, writes that the Greek word *splanchnizomai*, translated in the New Testament as "compassion," means to be "moved from the bowels," to feel the suffering of another in the depths of your being. Perhaps the next time we feel the need for some self-care we can take a moment to consider this. What if there is real grief for the world that we need to be addressing? Harper, a tireless advocate for justice, is also someone who can rock a good red lipstick and celebrate joy where she finds it. But she is adamant that Christians need to move away from charity and compassion work (individuals and communities giving out of their abundance) and toward community development and justice work, where oppressive systems and policies are changed. Instead of handing out sandwiches to hungry folks twice a week, what if a church helped start a food co-op in the community? This approach requires relationship, listening, and asking questions about the conditions that create hunger and food scarcity, and then changing those systems. Inherent in this type of work is the desire for justice, which can often look like privileged communities recognizing how they have been complicit or even profited from inequality.

As I sat at the Homeboy Cafe and ate that cinnamon roll dripping with frosting, surrounded by tourists and former gang members and neighborhood regulars, I realized something: self-care is not about numbing us from the realities of the world. Instead, it's about learning how to be resilient in the face of this glorious mess of fractured kinship we inherited from each other.

★ ★ ★

I think of the women I know who have experienced forced migration, who have survived the deaths of their families, their dreams, their cultures, their land. Who have and continue to scratch out their demand for dignity in a world that only wants to silence, demean, and other them. And I think of the countless feasts these women have made for me and others. I think of the joy taken in rice perfectly cooked, platters of nuts artfully arranged, a can of mango juice thrust into my hands the moment I take a seat on the couch. I have been changed by the hospitality I have received in the kitchens of apartments where people were starting over after their worlds had ended. I have had my sadness transformed into awe and gratitude by watching another move forward with resilience, even joy. They remind me to pay attention to delight.

I'm working these little muscles slowly. I notice cakes made with too much frosting and too many sprinkles. Children receiving free electric-green beanies at school one day and streaming home in a mass, looking like a burst of fireflies. My daughter absentmindedly twirling a curl of her hair as she giggles at the exploits of a Garfield cartoon. My son bursting into my room at 6 a.m., ready to start the day with a few minutes of snuggling. My husband texting me stupid jokes only we will get, the flush of insular and secret and solitary love. Dance parties to disco music, an inexplicable family favorite. Leaving Christmas lights up a little longer than necessary simply because they brighten the dark months. Petting my cat and marveling at the soft gray fur, the complexity of his eyes.

Living into this commitment will look different for everyone. It can mean creating more opportunities for feasting together or simply taking a moment to count your blessings before you fall asleep at night. Celebrating, even in the midst of injustice and pain, is a time-honored tradition of reimagining a new world by living into joy in the here and now with those who have been exiled as our guides. In the end we don't just want to dismantle the walls, the systems, the hierarchies, the exploitation in the world. We want to build something new, something centered on a kingdom that doesn't roll in with tanks but comes as a gigantic party: the wedding feast to end all feasts. What we all want is the happiest place on earth. Then, and only then, our kinship will finally be made real in the place where everyone, not just some, gets to experience the magic of the new creation.

PART FOUR

POWER

History will be kind to me because I intend to write it.

WINSTON CHURCHILL

20 ⋆ EMPIRE

I was in a chapel in Cambridge, surrounded by walls and pews and stained glass older than I can trace my family tree. I was unprepared for the grandeur of tradition that met me everywhere I went: the buildings and churches going back to the seventh century, the first bookstore in all of England, the plaques commemorating a famous scientist or theologian around every corner. A bright-eyed American in sensible shoes, I wandered the cobblestone streets gazing rapturously at all the glorious history I was experiencing.

There for a conference, I sat next to kindly old vicars who told me that less than 5 percent of people in England attend church, a drastic drop that had occurred in the last several decades. I was shocked to hear this, surrounded as we were on all sides by stately, ornate, historical churches. In every room we gathered, where we ate, where we worshiped even—large oil portraits hung on the walls. Famous men, men who were the academic deans or men who made great and important discoveries. Some of them with bushy white eyebrows and wild eyes, others sitting in severe armchairs, their hands clasped together. The Americans visiting like myself were puzzled by all the hagiography, slightly unnerved by the feeling of being watched by Great Men no matter where we went.

In the chapel at Magdalene College, I felt this connection at every turn. This is where Samuel Pepys went, this is the room where C. S. Lewis lived when he was a professor here for decades. The chapel was built in 1470, and I was in that room—I was connected to thousands and thousands of living, breathing, Christian witnesses. In front of me was an ancient Book of Common Prayer, musty and a little tattered looking. Upon opening the book, the first page showed it was published in 1754—terrified, I shut it quickly. Was I even allowed to touch something so ancient and hallowed?

But after a moment I opened the book again, and I prayed the prayers along with everyone around, thinking all the while about faith. My mind drifted to the beautiful stained-glass windows, their meanings inscrutable to me, the dust in the air catching the light. Mostly, I thought about what it means to thrive as a follower of Christ, even when by all accounts your religion has failed in the eyes of the watching world.

* * *

The Jewish people were primarily shaped by two stories: the exodus and the exile. Growing up evangelical in America, I was more familiar with the first story—Moses, the Red Sea, the wanderings in the desert, the Ten Commandments, the formation of a new chosen people. But Nick Page, a writer and theologian from the United Kingdom, says that many of us who are removed by both years and geography have largely forgotten about the exile part: how so many of the key works of the Old Testament were written in the shadow of trying to make sense of a terrible tragedy—Israel being taken into captivity by Babylon, the mark of a failed God and a failed religion.[1] Instead of assimilating God into the Babylonian story, the Israelites did something different from their peers: they fiercely held on to their stories and their belief in God, even as they lost their land, homes, and people.

How can we who are not exiled read these important narratives of faith in the midst of failure? It starts with understanding where we are in the story. If the Israelites have been shaped by exodus and exile, perhaps it is time to take a look at the other players in the story: those who have been shaped by empire. All empires—both in the biblical times and now—have a few characteristics in common, primarily the consolidation of military, economic, political, and ideological power. Throughout history the variety and strength of each of these characteristics fluctuate, but they are all present. Of increasing importance to me is that last category, the ideological or social might of the empire: the beliefs that empires propagate to keep and retain power. For instance, the belief that the empire will use that power for good (think *Pax Romana*, the ultimate benevolent empire slogan). Or the belief that the empire will never die.

I see the tendrils of these viewpoints in my own mind. Today I can see fractures both big and local in the American evangelical church, and still I won't believe in an ending. *American evangelicalism will live on, it will weather the storm of attaching itself to the pursuit of power at the cost of loving their neighbors. It cannot end.* This stubborn thought remains, and the quiet belief behind it is where the real power of empire lies: America, and more specifically White evangelical expressions of Christianity in America, cannot die because it is inherently blessed by God. This is ingrained in my brain, where this vicious myth has taken root and made itself true. This is how empire always works, by convincing us there is no other path forward except the one where we are always victorious. And this is how the narrative of empire is working, even now, in my own heart and soul and mind.

It isn't that I am anti-American, not really. As James Baldwin said, "I love America more than any country in the world, and exactly for this reason, I insist on the right to criticize her perpetually."[2] Empires are complicated structures; no matter where we live on this earth, we live with some sort of relationship to empire—and we need to figure out how to live as disciples of Christ right where we are. As a middle-class White American female, the dominant culture of the United States has been pretty good for me, which is important to articulate. I am someone who benefits from the empire at work around me, which means I have a spiritual and moral responsibility to interrogate the narratives that surround me. I need to seek out those who have experienced exodus and exile, and I need to contemplate what life beyond or in spite of empire might look like: contemplating the end of how everything always has been and supposedly always will be. There is nothing in Scripture, nothing in Jesus, that says my proud and terrible and interesting country is particularly blessed, has some special favor, has some special reason for existence.

Empire focuses on ideological sameness: make the narrative easy, make it clear. Pharaoh will save you. Caesar will put bread in your belly. The president will make our country great again. This leads to small, deformed imaginations—I see it in how White evangelical Christianity has been tangled up in the same pull toward greatness, toward power, toward viewing ourselves as specially anointed by God to rule the world, to hold and be in charge. This leads to a sense of scarcity, a hallmark of pharaohs throughout the centuries: the all-consuming fear of losing power. I have seen it in the fights for religious liberty that exclude those who aren't Christian, in the narrative that says we are losing the culture war and must fight with every tooth and nail to hold our ground, in scaring people to vote for certain candidates in order to maintain control. Undergirding these tactics is the belief that failure is not an option, that our ways will never die. But most important is the belief that exile is a reality to be ignored and feared at all costs, a strange ideological position for those who claim to follow the God of the Israelites.

★ ★ ★

The lovely Christians I met in Cambridge were true believers. Connected to the old ways, forging something new in the shadow of tradition and history. They had "lost" the culture, by most accounts, and yet they still remained a vibrant gathering of Christ-followers: smaller in number, perhaps, but with a bone-deep commitment to God's kingdom coming on earth as it was in heaven. Well-read, committed to studying Scripture and theology, we gathered together to pray as our ancestors did, all the good and the bad jumbled up. Ours was a history of marrying Christ with monarchies and empires and colonialism and imperialism; it was also a history of slouching toward Jesus that continues to live on to this day.

Perhaps more than ever Christians in the United States, especially those who come from dominant-culture backgrounds, are seriously starting to consider if their world really is going to change, of what it might look like to lose the coziness of partnership with empire. As we become ever more in the minority, as the locus of fresh and vibrant Christianity is found Latin America, Asia, and Africa, those of us who have been influenced by Great Men and Great Books and Great Theology of the mostly Western civilization kind will be experiencing a death of sorts. A failure that pales in comparison to Israel being captured by Babylon but feels like the pressure to assimilate or disperse all the same.

Many of my neighbors and friends are actual exiles—women from Muslim countries starting afresh here in my own neighborhood. Their faith is a constant for many of them, a space of solace and strength—for some, their faith actually grows stronger, richer, because now they are the minority. They need to know what they believe and why, because there are no cultural forces supporting them—in fact, oftentimes it is just the opposite. They have experienced the ending of their worlds and now show me what it is like to be in exile, to be faithful people in the midst of the apocalypse.

In an ancient chapel halfway around the world, I thought about these neighbors: their prayer rugs, the way they grieve with each other when life gets too hard, the way they show up to English class and birthday parties, how they have fresh-baked bread and spicy noodles for nearly every occasion. I held them in my mind in a chapel built in 1470, dedicated by a king who wanted all of his actions to be baptized by God. I thought about them as I ran my finger over the ancient Book of Common Prayer, as I sat in a seat in a chapel that for most of its history only let men inside, most of them White and European.

In 1988 Magdalene College was the last university in Cambridge to finally allow women to study in their hallowed halls. What feels like dying to some perhaps feels like the fresh winds of the Spirit to others. Tradition is beautiful but it is also five hundred-plus years of the doors to this hallowed space being only open for a few. It is me sitting in the chapel but surrounded by portraits hanging up in every hall of men who do not reflect me in my full humanity, nor the world in how it was designed to reflect the wondrously creative image of God.

In five hundred years what will my own people say? Where will we gather, and how will we worship the God who created us, loved us, died for us, resurrected for us? It's hard for me to say because my mind has been formed in the fear and longing for power that characterizes empire. I have little imagination for what life in exile could truly look like, I have little vision for a world in which faith flourishes even as church buildings crumble into disuse, or condos, or coffee shops. But I do know this: the world is changing, and we don't have to be afraid. We just might have to start looking elsewhere for where to go forward. We just might have to start learning to pray and sing and live in exile from those we have barred from entry for far too long.

21 ✶ BILLBOARDS

I ONCE HEARD that the 7-Eleven around the corner from my house, across the street from the apartments where we used to live, was the place you were most likely to get shot in all of Portland. It did not mean all that much to me until someone did die, a young man named Larnell Bruce Jr. He was nineteen years old, he was Black, and he was chased and run over repeatedly by two avowed White supremacists in a truck.

Our community was shaken, both by the violence itself and by its racially charged circumstances. Two White supremacists—a man and his girlfriend—in a truck, one Black man running for his life. Over the next few days and weeks, makeshift memorials were set up on the wall outside of the 7-Eleven. Spray-painted hearts and messages of love for Larnell. A teddy bear. Mylar balloons, shiny and silvery. I wanted to add something but felt as though my grief were displaced. I didn't know Larnell, and now I never would.

But still—it was my neighborhood, my corner store, my country's racial tensions demonstrated in this violent death. In a book of prayers put together by friends and fellow activists, I found a prayer specifically for this kind of event: a prayer for a death in the neighborhood. "For the unbearable toil of our sinful world, we plead for remission. For the terror of absence from our beloved, we plead for your comfort. For the scandalous presence of death in your Creation, we plead for resurrection."[1]

I went to the spot where Larnell had been murdered and awkwardly prayed this prayer. It didn't feel like enough. Eventually, the messages of love and remembrance were painted over—first in the bland beige of the surrounding store, then with a brightly colored mural. The mural, I suppose, was meant to evoke feelings of goodwill for our neighborhood—it showed the MAX train, buildings, and birds. In the center, a large tree with hearts all over the trunk, hearts with expressionless heads in varieties of black, brown, and white. I know it was supposed to make me feel better, but it didn't. It felt instead like it was telling a lie. It felt like that mural had painted over the truth.

* * *

Thomas Merton wrote about the two kinds of American myths that the White person needs to reckon with. Writing in the midst of the civil rights movement and the subsequent waves of racial violence perpetrated by White people in the 1960s, Merton said the two legacies to be dealt with were the plantation owners and the pioneers. As someone who lives in the Pacific Northwest, I feel comfortable with the first category because I am comfortable vilifying people from other parts of my country who profited off of explicit racial injustice like chattel slavery. The plantation owner narrative does not pierce me because I view it as so separate and far away from me. I do not feel indicted or implicated. In fact, mulling over their sins makes me feel better about myself.

But it is the other category that Merton introduces, the pioneers, where things get a bit more slippery. As Merton knew, the pioneer mythology is more complex, more discreet, less likely to be challenged with an uproar. And yet the threads of oppression that run through the narrative of chattel slavery are also present in the pioneer narrative. The pioneer takes, the pioneer owns, the pioneer is viewed as first when really they were just had better weaponry. They are the outsider perpetually proud.

But just as you can't have a plantation owner without enslaved persons, you can't have a God-ordained pioneer without the idea of "savages" to be conquered. To truly begin to view and then dismantle both of the myths of White supremacy—the plantation owner and the pioneer—we first need to question the structures and beliefs that uphold them. My friend Melissa asked me this once: who pays for our myths? I want to ask myself that question nearly every day. Every time I wake up in my house, when I walk the streets of my neighborhood. Who pays for my cherished identity as a pioneer—as good and deserving, as outside, yet also benefiting from these power structures? Who pays for our inner beliefs? Who benefits? And who, in the end, gets to tell that story?

* * *

One day I noticed a billboard in my neighborhood, a few blocks away from the 7-Eleven. It showed a White man in a cowboy hat squinting into the camera. The crows' feet around his eyes are deep, and his face is tanned and pleasingly worn. Like the Marlboro Man, everything about the image is telling us that this fellow is a man's man, an iconic American. He's earned his way in the American frontier. There is a logo for Coors, the brewing company, on the right, and in large font it says, "Out here, we answer to no one."

I went back to my house and felt compelled to learn more about the history of the company and the message on the large board in my neighborhood. Coors was built in Colorado by immigrants from Europe over a century ago. As the company grew, so did the mystique—the founders refused to sell their beer in the majority of the country, focusing only the West, adding to the mythology (people on the East Coast in particular found it had a certain Western cachet). Their brand is built on rugged thirst, beautiful mountains, cold cans of beer—masculinity married with a sense of freedom and ownership. Selling the pioneer myth to a neighborhood of immigrants and refugees and people displaced by rising housing costs, selling the myth to people who experienced violence and tragedy, who constantly were expected and needed to answer to each other.

I kept digging, discovering that controversies surround the company in later years, including large-scale boycotts by Chicano labor activists and LGBTQ groups for workplace discrimination, while the Colorado Civil Rights Commission found that Coors discriminated against Black employees repeatedly in the 1970s. The Coors family itself responded by becoming increasingly opposed to government regulation, expanding on the pioneer mentality. Joe Coors, son of the original founder, believes that "the government which governs the least governs the best," at least when it comes to suit him and his business needs.[2] Self-described as an "ultrapatriot," Joe Coors went on to help fund and form the Heritage Foundation, the most influential conservative think tank in American politics (from Nixon to Trump; Trump leans heavily on nominations from Heritage to staff his White House).[3] The Heritage Foundation works to uphold free enterprise and limit government regulation while promoting "traditional American values." For conservative think tanks, the Heritage Foundation has been hailed as a "pioneering effort." But what precisely are they pioneering?

I thought about my research every time I saw that billboard in my neighborhood. That pioneer man, those crinkly eyes, that message: out here, we answer to no one. And the questions began to bubble up, a sour spring within my heart: Who benefits from this particular myth? And who ultimately will pay the price?

★ ★ ★

Across the street from the Coors man there's another billboard that went up a few months ago. I was walking my children home from the library when I saw it and gasped aloud. It showed a picture of a Black boy in a football uniform posing for a school portrait, one knee up, a small smile on his face. Below it were the words: "21 white supremacist groups active in Oregon." At the bottom, in much smaller letters, it read, "Live and Love Larnell Bruce Jr."

I said his name over and over again in my head as I walked my children the few blocks home. I had only seen the photos of Larnell used in news reports when he was older, wearing a dark-colored jacket, unsmiling, looking like an adult instead of the teenager that he was. This billboard was another view of his humanity, one designed to be reckoned with. Then there was that number, the number of White supremacist groups active and engaged in Oregon. Once I might have felt shock or terror at that number—twenty-one groups, in 2018, in a supposedly progressive state—but now I felt weary with recognition of the reality.

The organization that put up the billboard about Larnell Bruce Jr. is called Portland Equity in Action. For three months they put up billboards all over the city designed to address the complacency and racial disparity in Portland—from signs that said "Black Lives Matter" to "Your White Fragility Is Showing" to "Who Is Allowed the Presumption of Innocence?" Whenever I saw one of their billboards, especially on the outer east side of the city, I felt a thrill of sorts. This is what slogans are designed to do—to get a reaction, to spark conversation, to push back against the narrative that all is well in Portland.

But it was the billboard closest to my house, a few blocks past the 7-Eleven, that always stopped me cold. I always wondered if my kids would notice it tucked up between the large daycare center and the Taco Time. My daughter, going into the third grade, tried to walk while reading at the same time, something I used to do at her age. She wandered down the sidewalk, past homeless people sleeping in the doorways of an old Grange Hall, past a pawn shop with huge pictures of gold coins and dollar bills. She walked, confident that I would direct her if she strayed too far away. Above us, Larnell Bruce Jr. kneeled in his football uniform. I don't know how old he was in that picture, but he was on the cusp of no longer being viewed by American society as a gorgeous child (if indeed he ever was valued as such). Perhaps the second he got up from that pose and took off his uniform, he became the threat that so many wanted to say he was.

But as the billboard made clear, Larnell Bruce—Larnell Bruce Jr.: he was somebody's son, don't ever forget that—he is not responsible for his own death. It's the large lettering and that large number that looms a shadow over my heart. Twenty-one active White supremacist organizations in Oregon, simmering both under and over the surface of our supposed progressive utopia. They are the ones we need to answer for. They are made up of some of our brothers and uncles and church members and coworkers. The problem is not only that Larnell Bruce Jr. is dead. The problem is that my neighbors killed him, that they continue to live marinated in an ideology that has an extensive network of roots and vines tunneling throughout the American landscape: an ideology that needs to subsume, to consume, to silence in order to thrive.

★ ★ ★

I can walk around my neighborhood and see trucks with the Confederate flag on them, trucks with "Redneck Nation" emblazoned on the back, houses with "Don't Tread on Me" flags and "I Don't Call 911" signs with an image of a gun pointing straight at me, the reader. I see symbols of violence everywhere I look, decals of guns and staking claim and territory, trucks gunning up and down the busy streets, huge American flags whipping by in the air, almost always driven by White men. I look at them and feel afraid, and then resolve not to. That's what they want people to feel. I stare at their bumper stickers, their flags, their symbols that lay claim to their rights above the rights of others. When I feel the fear rise up, I pray it away. I pray blessings on those men, and I pray the same thing for both of us: Lord, take our fear and replace it with love.

I often walk by the mural that was painted at the 7-Eleven by my house, a makeshift billboard of a kind. The mural was designed to make people feel better about the spot where Larnell Bruce Jr. was murdered. But when I see it—the faceless people of different hues, the hearts, the tree a symbol of our interconnectedness—I do not feel like we are one happy family. I feel like maybe the mural was painted to stop people from spray painting a specific name on the wall. When I look at those black and brown and white hearts floating up an imaginary tree of life, they do not comfort me. Whoever painted it, and whoever paid them to do it, contributed to the erasure of Larnell Bruce Jr.'s name and life and death. It is cheerful, beautiful, and glosses over the truth of my neighborhood. Whenever I walk past the 7-Eleven with my children, the colors of the paint catching their eyes, I want to point out to them how significant it is. I want to tell them this mural was designed to silence lament in the name of false peace.

We walk to the library, to the store, to school. And I want to teach them with every step that if they only pay attention, they'll see billboards everywhere they look whose purpose to try to make us forget who does and does not pay for the sins of the pioneers.

22 ★ THE PIONEER MIND

Just then North America was discovered, as if it had been kept in reserve by the Deity and had risen just beneath the waters of the Deluge. From the perilous beginning on the shores of a wilderness continent, the United States of America has become a leader of nations and the bastion of freedom for the world. . . . God, in His wisdom, allowed America to remain hidden until the Modern Age had dawned in Europe, bringing with it a number of important changes that would profoundly affect the course of American history.

ALEXIS DE TOCQUEVILLE

I GREW UP ON THE LITTLE HOUSE ON THE PRAIRIE books; I grew up longing to be like Laura Ingalls, who never was a good little girl, and found myself identifying with her family and their rootless pioneer ways. My mother unschooled my sisters and me before it was a trend—we wandered the fields and read whatever books made our brains light up, with little structure or demands on our time. One year she read us the Little House on the Prairie books and little else. It was my favorite year of school (except for the disgusting acorn pancakes we harvested, ground, and ate ourselves).

My own daughter doesn't care about Laura Ingalls; she is interested in magic and cats and Malala and Harry Potter. Still, one right of parenthood is trying desperately to convince our kids to like the things we did—but when I tried to reread the Little House books to her I was troubled by the easy slips into colonialism, paternalism, and downright hostility toward the original inhabitants of the land that dotted the pages. In my memory the titular prairie was wide and empty, awaiting the Ingalls family to wrestle it into submission. This, of course, is not true, but it is how the mind of a little girl who comes from people like the Ingallses would think. To baptize my imagination and that of my daughter as well, I picked up a different book to read to her at night: *The Birchbark House*, a book about a little Anishinabe girl named Omakayas, a fictional contemporary of Laura Ingalls.[1] The Birchbark House series follows Omakayas throughout the seasons of a year, how her family survives trials and tribulations, their connection to each other, the land, the seasons. It is tragic and funny and never, ever boring. My daughter was enthralled. She did not know that the author, Louise Erdrich, an indigenous woman, wrote it so other people like herself could see themselves mirrored in stories without the gaze of the pioneer. All my daughter knew is that it was a very good story. When I finished the last page she sighed happily. "I wish that story would never end," she said, and I agreed with her.

We will keep reading these stories together. I still keep the Little House on the Prairie books because one day my daughter might like to read them, and one day we might talk about who wrote them and why they viewed the world as they did. It is no good pretending like all the histories that have already been written don't exist. For me, someone who is the child of pioneers with the mind of pioneers, I have a different task: to seek and find the other histories. To seek and celebrate the stories we were taught to ignore, erase, or dismiss. This is the first step in acknowledging that how we see ourselves in the world is not always correct. It is the first step of acknowledging that people who come from places of power and privilege always see ourselves as the center.

* * *

When I did read Christian history textbooks at home, they told me America was a pristine wilderness until it was discovered by Europeans. They told me the US Constitution was sacred, as are the Founding Fathers who worked hard to give rights to all. The Civil War was unfortunate, not because of slavery but because it splintered our great nation. The problems of our modern age are worse than ever, the books concluded, and nearly all of them stem from the ideas of humanists and liberals. The great sin of our age is that we Americans have not returned to our hallowed, God-ordained roots. In the textbooks I read, in the homeschool groups I was a part of, in the radio programs we listened to, and the historical novels we read, I absorbed a persistent imperative to do my part: to return Christians in America to our former political, social, and cultural power, and to make America what it once was. And before the Civil War, America was most certainly great.[2]

This is the worldview I was born into, and we called it the Christian worldview. For my community it was a way of seeing and living in the world based on the Bible and supposedly not through the lenses of secular culture. For my parents and many others this meant gravitating toward Christian curriculum that contained no atheism, evolutionary theory, or secular humanism. Only God and the Bible and a commonsense understanding of both. This particular form of biblicism—focused on a literal interpretation of Scripture that had only become popularized in the last few hundred years—coincided with an urge to retreat from the world that was intent on harming, shaming, or indoctrinating us.[3] Because of this, here has been a slow and steady rise in homeschooling or educating children in private Christian schools or pursuing "classical" Christian education for the past few decades in the United States. I've often wondered about this. Why was there suddenly such a need for a different way of viewing the world? Why was there suddenly such a drastic need for separation, for educating children separate from the society at large? When did Christians give up on evangelizing their fellow neighbors and start to plan for how to be separate, superior, and more righteous?

I used to joke about being a fundamentalist because I was so sure I was not—I didn't wear overall dresses or keep my hair long, and I didn't read the King James Version of the Bible only. I have been sobered to realize the ideology of fundamentalism from the nineteenth and twentieth centuries carries forth into my life today. In looking at history I see how forms of evangelicalism became suspicious of modernity—including science, the media, and popular culture. In terms of education and curriculum, independent Christian schools began to grow in earnest in the 1960s, suspiciously right around the time that desegregation laws went into effect. In the 1990s homeschooling became more a popular (and more economical) choice with three curriculums—ACE, Bob Jones, and Abeka—being the most readily available, and used by Christians from a wide variety of backgrounds and denominations. But the thread of segregation remains an important undercurrent—all three of these popular publishers had their roots in Bob Jones University, a fundamentalist college in South Carolina that prides itself on its biblical literalism and lack of moral compromise.[4] My parents did not fully understand the roots of this ideology, and neither did I. Nor did we understand the full scope of the curriculum or the desire behind it. We thought we were being faithful.

To be a good a Christian, we were told, was to focus on our own families, to keep them protected from the world, and to raise them up to be leaders. We were to be paragons of virtue and education, removed and pristine. We were being trained to take over the position of power and to embrace the idea that this was a directive from God himself. The world, like America before the arrival of White Protestants, was a place of chaos and confusion, destined—when the time was right—to be colonized, to be brought into godly order. We were meant to carry on the great traditions that were a part of America's founding story and to claim this land for God. We were to take and use power for good.

Scholars call this "dominion theology"—that God wants Bible-believing Christians to be in control of the United States government and in other places of power. Dominion theology is often associated with the works of the conservative Calvinist thinker Rousas John Rushdoony, who was invested in the Old Testament biblical law codes and seeing them—all of them—reinstated. Other Christian have adopted Rushdoony's views to varying degrees, including people like Bob Jones, James Dobson, and Francis Schaeffer. The goal was the same: to train conservative Christians to take up influential positions in the world, uncorrupted by the evils of modernity and liberalism, and to return America once more to the biblical morality that is supreme above all others.

Willie Jennings has perhaps done more work than any current theologian to unpack the seeds of this thinking: how European Protestant expansionism has paved the way for our current reality, where whiteness is forever bound up in the story of the expansion Christianity and the story of the United States. Jennings explains how the concept of race and racial hierarchy was formed by White Europeans as they ventured into the new world and came into contact with a wide array of new peoples, cultures, and customs. The Europeans asked the question, Who am I in this strange new place? Jennings writes that the question itself is not bad, but the answer revealed the sin and selfishness of the European explorers. Am I a conqueror or the conquered? The conquistadors and explorers created a racial hierarchy that contrasted themselves with the new lands: White was on top, followed by people from Asia and Latin America, and people from Africa were relegated to the bottom and designated Black.

One overlooked and devastating element of this history is how the conquistadors baptized their enslavement of other peoples with the belief that they were spreading Christianity. Jennings writes about a Portuguese scribe named Zarura who struggled to come to terms with his official role describing the history of the Portuguese king as God's will while also gazing on the first Black slaves brought to his country and their fear, terror, and distress. Zarura cries, even, Jennings points out—"I pray Thee that my tears may not wrong my conscience; for it is not their religion but their humanity that maketh mine to weep in pity for their sufferings."[5] Zarura knows that these families—who will be separated, torn apart, and become slaves for the rest of their lives and their children's lives—are human beings "born of Adam" and that their suffering is real and terrifying, implicating himself and his countrymen. But Jennings points out that this is where Zarura wrestles with the problem of theodicy—the reality of evil and sin in the world—

and conflates it with the expansion of both the Portuguese Empire and the Christian religion. Jennings writes that ultimately Zarura helps pen and promote a new way of viewing the world through the lens of the conquerors: how "divine immutability yields Christian character—an unchanging God wills to create Christians out of slaves and slaves out of those Black bodies that will someday, the Portuguese hope, claim to be Christian."[6] This is what the dominant Christian imagination rests on, says Jennings. It is a diseased imagination, one centered in the privileged making sense of their place in the world and the suffering they exact from others. And God, of course, must be on their side. Providence was always on the side of the victor, it was always on the side of those who claimed to know God, and it was always on the side of those who ended up writing the narratives.

★ ★ ★

The diseased imagination shows up prominently in the high school history textbooks I grew up on, copies of which I bought on eBay to peruse for myself. It was worse than I remembered, but perhaps that is because I am an adult now, and not an impressionable child. The call to take back the country, to Make America Great Again, is a familiar song that I never knew I was singing my whole life. The focus on the books like the ones I grew up on love to talk about the good examples: Confederate general Robert E. Lee, they said "displayed the admirable characteristics of leadership, humility, compassion, and dedication to duty" while his fellow Confederate general Stonewall Jackson was "a military genius and a great Christian . . . who organized large and successful Sunday schools for slaves."[7]

I was supposed to long to be in power and to believe that I would wield it for good and for God. I was supposed to grow strong and smart and confident in my worldview and to vote for people just like me to take the country back again. But this didn't happen to me. My parents introduced me to too many diverse groups of people, encouraged me to read the actual words of Jesus one too many times. In adolescence I started to have serious problems reconciling the Suffering Servant with a conservative political agenda. I started to wonder how to practically implement Jesus' stories and commandments into my actual life, how to love my wildly disparate neighbor as myself. The more I came into contact with people who didn't grow up exactly like me, the more the lenses of my Christian worldview began to become visible. I started to believe that the biblical ethic is not about being safe or in power or even being removed from the world. Instead, the Bible seems to show us the radical love of God and for God's desire that we should live out sacrificial neighbor love.

When I was young I read quotes like this, molding my imagination in chilling ways:

> Native Americans, like most early people, forsook the things they once knew about God. Rather than worshipping the Creator, they worshipped creation, particularly things they could not understand such as thunder, wind, fire, and the sun. . . . Because superstition kept the Indians from working together to develop the land on which they lived, America would remain an untamed wilderness until the Europeans arrived.[8]

Instead of celebrating connections to the land, here it is juxtaposed as the antithesis to loving the true God, and it proves the pioneers were right to erase the people and the narratives before them in the name of Christian expansionism.

I remember these textbooks and what they taught me about America as I look at the yellowed box set of the complete Little House on the Prairie books slowly moldering on my daughter's shelf. They are there to read should she ever care to open them, and together we will talk about why Ma was so scared or why Pa thought the world was his to claim. My daughter and I will try to seek out new stories together that bear witness to the ones for whom Christianity coupled with empire have not often been good news. For now we sink into the Birchbark House books; we imagine the world of Omakayas and her connection to the seasons, to bears and fish and berries, surviving in a world fraught with complicity. We do this because we learn about our own impoverished viewpoint by being absorbed into the story of someone we had formerly erased.

The antidote to these myths is to consciously remember those who are not writing the history textbooks. To pay attention to the world, and the myths we promote and the histories we ignore. To seek out the stories that do not just celebrate people like us but that remember those who came first. We are never as free from the histories of pain and suffering as we'd like to be. Power is never as good or as clean or as simple as we think. The pioneer myth says that the one who wins, the one who survives gets all the glory and riches. At some point followers of Christ who live with such an ideology have to choose whether they believe it or if they might be willing to entertain the idea that they've been asked to lay down their rights and enter into a space that is neither barren nor empty nor pristine—the world, beautifully inhabited, full of people already here—and learn to live in it as neighbors instead of conquerors.

23 ★ SIGNPOSTS

When we moved into our house around the corner from the apartment complex where we used to live, I put up a sign in the front yard that said, No Matter Where You're From, We're Glad You Are Our Neighbor, in three different languages: English, Spanish, and Arabic. My motives, as ever, were mixed. I wanted to love others in a way that is easy and still makes me feel good. I'm the type of person who loves to display my values on a sign in front of the house—a house I could afford to buy in part because of my privileged position in society.

Our neighborhood is a microcosm of the way our cities are going, the next wave of gentrification. Places like Portland, San Francisco, and Seattle have attracted throngs of tech workers and wealthy businesses, inviting them to "revitalize" and reclaim the urban cores of cities. As more people move in, drawn to amenities like walkability and art and culture, the rents have raised accordingly. Lower-income folks, those who work the service jobs that prop up a city, are pushed farther and farther out. Since these workers can no longer afford to live in the neighborhoods they grew up in, they're pushed into the surrounding suburbs—places that were never intended for them but are still more affordable than the city center And now, as the wealthy work to revitalize the urban core, the property values of just a few decades prior are turned upside down, the low-income folks finding themselves with no option but to live in what remains, a place that was never intended for them: the suburbs.

White flight, or the phenomenon of White people leaving the inner core of the cities to the suburbs, is a relatively well-known phenomenon. But now, as the city continues to be seen as more desirable—indeed, as Christians have started to declare God's love for the city and God's desire to "reclaim" the cities—the reverse trend is happening, what has been called "the great inversion."[1]

For the first time in US history, the majority of poor people in metropolitan regions live in the suburbs. This has of course disproportionately affected people of color and people who have lived in generational poverty in the United States, but it has also affected another population: immigrants and to a lesser extent refugees, who used to be resettled in the urban core where rents were cheap. Now, they almost always move to the suburbs, the only places where rent is affordable.

This is where I live, now. The apartment buildings in my own neighborhood are filled to the brim with people of color displaced from North Portland, with immigrant and White families trying to squeak by. The houses, many of them built in the 1950s, still are mostly owned by White people; older folks who are trying to sell now that the market is good and the demographics have shifted. The homeowners, people who have been here for a long time, are not necessarily happy about the changes they've seen in the past few decades as low-income families have streamed into the neighborhood. There's tension in the air, in the streets, in the school—palpable but still mostly underground.

When I first put my sign up in the yard, I felt a bit nervous. How would people react? I wasn't surprised when a few months after we put the sign up in our yard it was purposely run over by a car. Bent and dirty, it was still usable, and I felt a grim satisfaction as I stuck it back in the yard, proud of my tolerance. A few weeks later and it was gone—it had been stolen. Who had done this? I tried to imagine what sort of person would steal a welcome sign. In my mind's eye the thief was someone I didn't like, someone I feared slightly. But this someone, I realized, was also my neighbor. How was I supposed to learn to love them when a simple welcome sign was perceived as a threat?

At a recent neighborhood association meeting I attended, an older White woman asked a police officer why they didn't do more about the "bad" people who were committing crimes. The officer admitted that they were understaffed and overwhelmed. This woman declared that our neighborhood needed more police officers and that if it was up to her, she would "take care of" the bad guys. When she said this, this old woman, wearing a pastel-colored sweater, her head full of white hair, made her fingers into the shape of a gun and pantomimed shooting somebody. The police officer shook his head ruefully and laughed. I gasped and a few heads swiveled around to look at me. "That's a pretty hard-core approach," the police officer said, "but I see where you're coming from." Later, he told the room of neighborhood residents that if he had his dream wish, they would expand the jails and open up a thousand more beds to keep more people inside. I felt small and hysterical, longing for a world where we had more imagination to think beyond guns and jail cells for the troubles of our world. I looked around the room, waiting for someone to contradict these narratives. Nobody else spoke up, and my own voice felt silenced by fear and despair.

In that room, a room set up for us to talk about our community, one of my neighbors wanted to kill some of my other neighbors. What would Jesus have me do in this situation? How do you love your neighbors when some of them have had fear curdle their hearts, when violence appears to them to be the best solution? What do you do when some of that despair and anger starts to rub off on you?

★ ★ ★

My friend Zeynab called me one day and told me to come to her apartment. When I got there, it was warm, both from something bubbling on the stove and from the five of us in her small apartment—my friend, her three children, and me. Zeynab laughed nervously and twisted her headscarf in her fingers. She wanted to tell me something. Earlier that day, she said, when she was coming back from English class with two of her children, she had been spat on by a man in a car.

I was shocked and expressed my dismay and sorrow. She laughed again, waving her hands. I am fine, she told me. She was waiting to cross the busy intersection that separated the bus stop from her apartment building. She was yards away from safety, the rental apartment that she has turned into a haven for her family. She told me that the man had yelled at her, waving his arms, hitting his steering wheel, his face red. He told her to go back home, several times.

Neither of us said anything, but I wonder if Zeynab was thinking it: if only she could go home. If only her home was safe for her and her family. But it wasn't, and she was here, which also wasn't safe. Zeynab brushed off all of my questions and dismissed my desire to report the incident. Instead, she told me a story. Allah, she said, plants all sorts of vegetation in the jungle, both good plants and bad plants, and they are in every country in the world, both her first country and in this place, her new country. Both good plants and bad plants, together they grow everywhere, you cannot have a world with just one kind.

The man in the car must not understand the Christian religion, she told me, because Miriam (Mary), the mother of Jesus, wore a headscarf. And if Mary wore a headscarf, why would Zeynab's headscarf be so upsetting to him? I listened to Zeynab laugh off her pain and fear. I listened to the stories she told to make sense of a world that was rarely safe for her. She was my teacher that day, a theologian explaining a faith that had been forged in the crucible of a world that was intent on crushing her, pushing her out, destroying her home, and then insisting she go back to it.

She told me she was not afraid, that she was fine, but I could tell otherwise. For weeks afterward she stayed inside her apartment instead of taking the bus to English class. But that man and his fear and hatred did not keep her down for long. Within a month I saw her again, crossing the street with her children clutching her hands, bound and determined to be a good seed no matter where God chose to plant her.

I now try to be more aware of power as I walk through my neighborhood and as I pray over the people. I try to be aware of who is afraid and where that fear is coming from: Are they afraid of their power being taken away, or do they fear for their safety? I try to address the thump of fear in my own heart as I hear stories of hatred. I try to pay attention to the anguish I feel instead of rushing to give into anger, despair, and cynicism. I try to lament, as best as I am able. I walk past Confederate flags and looming developments of high-priced condos, past needles on the ground and people screaming at each other. It's a discipline to remember that God is present, that God is love, even in those moments.

When I'm with Zeynab, I listen to her share her stories. There's no way to make the world a truly safe place for her, no way to flip the structures of the world on their head and put her at the top, with all the power. All I can do is listen, be present, let her be my host and my educator. I can begin to unlearn my desire to fix every problem quickly and efficiently. I can learn to be sad with someone as a manifestation of neighbor love.

★ ★ ★

Mark Charles once pointed out how a popular sign for progressives made him upset. This sign is in the style and colors of an American flag. It says, "In our America: All people are equal. Love wins. Black lives matter. Immigrants and refugees are welcome," and on and on. Charles, a member of the Navajo nation who has done significant research on the doctrine of discovery as it relates to Christian theology and the treatment of indigenous people in the United States, says that the fundamental problem with the sign is that it isn't true. The America where people are all equal, where love wins, where Black lives are treated as equally under the law as White lives, where policies and procedures exist to welcome immigrants and refugees into our country in ways they deserve—it's all a fantasy. And simply declaring it to be true doesn't change this.[2]

I know this because of my experiences in my own neighborhood and the stories carefully shared with me. What does it mean to put up a sign that speaks to a longing for another world? I think it is a place to start, but not the end goal. What we want is the imagination to believe in heaven coming down to earth, in God's will being done to our neighbors, to shalom being experienced by those who have and are suffering the most. And this will not happen until we change the systems that actually created and uphold the way the United States works, the way America actually is, and until we own it as our own. Deeply flawed, full of promise—if it is to ever be any good, then we will have to listen to those people who have been forced to perfect the democracy, as Nikole Hannah Jones says: the Black and indigenous and immigrant and LGBTQ+ and poor voices that have struggled to fight for their rights, to fight for the America that is supposedly good for all.[3]

After Zeynab told me about the man who spat on her, I walked around the corner to my house wishing as usual that I could make the world a better place with my good intentions and my own two hands. A few days later my neighbor across the street called out to me. He has a gentle demeanor and a large mustache; on Christmas Eve his family hosts elaborate parties, complete with large white tents and mariachi bands. His family is part of the small but growing number of non-White homeowners in our neighborhood. They are the kind of neighbors who keep to themselves, always smiling and waving. But this day my neighbor called out to me, so I went over to talk to him.

"Did you take your sign down?" he asked me. "Because I really liked it." Confused, I tilted my head. "The sign, in your front yard. Did you take it down?" I suddenly remembered. "No," I told him, "somebody stole it." He looked at me and squinted. "Oh," he said. "Well, I liked it. As soon as you put it up I knew we could trust you."

I remembered how nervous I felt about putting that sign up, the anger and cynicism that flared in me when it was vandalized and then taken for good. But I hadn't considered that it might do what it actually purported to do: that it could be a sign of welcome, that it could make even one person or family feel just the tiniest bit safer. I immediately went online, ordered another sign, and put it back up in my yard, where it stands to this day. If and when it gets taken, I will buy another one and another one, until the good Lord calls us to another home, either in this world or the next.

When someone tells you that the little flare you sent out into the world, hoping to find connection and true peace, hoping to find places of God's love and hospitality in the world, became a spark in the dark night sky for them, you take it seriously. It's never enough, of course. But it is a part of cultivating a holy imagination. A sign as a means of connecting to others, of tendrils going out to cultivate a good garden, of looking for others to partner with in the business of contributing to a flourishing neighborhood. When someone tells you that these signs mean something, then you keep sending up those flares until all of God's children one day are welcomed as neighbors with joy and gladness, until the sky is finally filled with that light.

24 ★ MONUMENTS AND MEMORIALS

In 1995 I decided I was a Jesus freak. I remember the moment it happened: in a huge stadium filled with people gathered together to hear Billy Graham, well into his seventies by then but still considered a rock star in my world. DC Talk was the opening act, playing an intoxicating mix of rock with a hint of hip hop, the lyrics all about being outside of popular culture and celebrating the fact, even if it meant facing persecution. I remember the altar call at the end of the evening, the thousands of people streaming down to the stage to say yes to Jesus. As my family got in our car and headed home, the line of cars waiting to leave the arena seemed endless, as many headlights as there were stars in the sky. I was eleven years old but I already knew I was a part of something special, true, and worthy of joining, but I was also prepared to fight for it, to expect to be on edge for the rest of my days as I battled to convince the rest of the world of the rightness of my cause.

In the ensuing years I embraced this mantra wholeheartedly. One of my most on-brand moments occurred when I was thirteen years old and started an evangelistic punk rock band, conscripting my older sister and several boys from the youth group to tour Northern California to try to convert people. I cut my hair short and bleached it blond and wore dog collars around my neck, but inside I was as pietistic as a Puritan housewife. When we were interviewed by the local paper, I was thrilled to see a photo of myself, looking seriously into the camera, with a quote: "Christians can be punk rockers too." With every simplistic bass line, with every tortured lyric about God (which maybe could have been interpreted to be about my sister's boyfriends), with every show we played in church basements, I was thrilled. I was a freak for Jesus. And I would do my part to be in the revolution without caving in to the identity of the world.

In an age of increasingly secular states (as opposed to the religious empires of previous centuries), professor Matthew Kaemingk suggests that there are four responses available to religious minorities when it comes to approaching power in a pluralistic society: assimilation, moderation, retreat, and retribution.[1] I grew up believing we were retreating from the world, but now I wonder if it wasn't really all about retreating in order to come back and be in charge someday (retribution). I was raised in a time of American evangelicalism where though we held enormous enclaves of power, we believed we were exiles in our own land. We were Protestants from a line of people who felt they had lost the culture war way back in the early twentieth century, we had retreated into our sanctuaries and seminaries and arena concerts and crusades (all places of power, it should be noted) to lick our wounds and shore up the faith.

This underdog theology remains powerful today, even as it is patently untrue. White evangelicals in particular regularly bemoan how the liberal media or Hollywood or social media is against them. I often think about what our situation would look like to the early followers of Jesus. The disciples, the writers of the Gospels, Paul himself would never be able to conceive of a world or society like America where (mostly White) Christians owned so many businesses, homes, wealth, institutions, and held the highest level positions of power in the government. We might be considered freaks in a different regard. We might be seen as the most preposterous of all: the people with power constantly stoking the fear that we will lose it, claiming the blessing of a Savior who urged us to do just that.

★ ★ ★

When you are raised to fear the loss of power, it can twist how you approach lament. I will never forget how someone I loved very much once calmly explained to me why an unarmed Black boy deserved to be killed and why his killer deserved to be acquitted by the legal system. This person told me this with very little emotion in their voice, speaking to me as if I was a child. And in a way I did feel like a child at that moment, a child who realizes in an instant that the world is not fair. I tried to argue my points in a cool and calculated manner, but instead I found myself crying almost to the point of screaming. I wailed as if I were at a funeral, and in a way I was. In a time when the television news seemed to show an endless succession of Black bodies left bleeding on the ground while their murderers walked free, I wailed as I watched so many people around me dismiss the sufferings of other people, time and time again. I watched as the people who raised me to expect injustice against our religion calmly accepted the systems that targeted other people. I wailed as I realized that people who loved God can also love systems that lead to death, especially if they remain free from those same terrors.

I have come to this realization later in life because of my own privilege: my white skin and middle-class upbringing, being surrounded by other people who felt safe expressing their religion constantly. But still I am puzzled over this juxtaposition: Christians who believe in the fall and yet when it comes to institutions like the American legal system or Christian universities or the police force, they act as if they are beyond the corruptions common to us all (depending on who is in charge or what issue is in question). William Stringfellow, a Harvard-educated lawyer and lay theologian in the 1960s, experienced his own conversion in this area. He had long thought the American legal system was both civil and fair. Even when he was prosecuted for helping his friend, the Jesuit priest Daniel Berrigan, evade arrest (for burning draft cards during the Vietnam War), he gave the system the benefit of the doubt (Stringfellow eventually had all charges dropped, confirming his trust).

But as Stringfellow went through life, as he entered into relationships with people who were different from himself, he started to question his trust in the system, the system he had dedicated his very life to. He learned about people like George Jackson, a Black man who went to prison due to a contested charge against him for stealing $70, served twelve years, and died there. Stringfellow soon learned that George Jackson wasn't an aberration. In fact, Stringfellow wrote in 1965, he now realized that "for blacks in the USA the law, in a quite overwhelming sense, in the legislature, in the courts, in law enforcement, and administration is now, as it always has been, an enemy: a harasser, an invader, an oppressor." Stringfellow takes this conclusion one step further and asks a question, one that I believe more people from privileged backgrounds need to ask themselves. "If the American legal system seems viable for me and other white Americans but is not so for citizens who are black, or for any others, then how, as the dual commandment would ask, in the name of humanity, can it be affirmed as viable for me or for any human being?"[2] In other words, if a system works for you but not for everyone, then how can we continue to view that system as just? Once we begin to understand that we have benefited from the same system that has crushed others, how can any follower of Christ accept this reality as a part of God's plan? We can't, says Stringfellow. We must recognize it for what it is, a principality and a power, a demonic system that leads to death. And we must learn to resist it. We pay attention. We listen to others. We tell the truth. And we learn to lament the reality in order to make way for a better future.

★ ★ ★

I was in a room lined with glass jars, each one filled to the brim with brown and gold and mahogany soil, jars on shelves that stretched all the way up to the tall ceiling. It was visually striking, and when I leaned in to look at the jars more closely I saw a date and location etched into each one. I recoiled slightly in horror as I realized what these jars were. They were soil collections from just a sampling of the known lynching sites on record in the state of Alabama. They were a testament to the earth and the blood that was spilt, an image of a history that had been made invisible to me.

The room was just one part of a museum and monument in Montgomery, Alabama, put together by the Equal Justice Initiative. The Equal Justice Initiative is led by Bryan Stevenson, a Harvard-educated lawyer who worked for decades with wrongfully convicted people on death row, the vast majority African American. After doing this work for decades, Stevenson realized that nothing would change if the underlying narrative of White supremacy didn't change. And he believes that the best way to change the narrative is to ask America to engage with its history of racial terror in meaningful ways: to lament the past in order to move forward into the future.[3]

Those jars of soil I saw in a room in Montgomery changed me. I went back to my beloved Pacific Northwest wondering what stories had been buried, wondering how I might need to connect myself to them. I discovered that there was only one lynching of a Black man on record in Oregon, in a coastal town in southern Oregon. His name was Alonzo Tucker, and he was lynched for allegedly having a relationship with a White woman. One bright summer day my entire family—my husband, two kids, and me—went on a pilgrimage of sorts to find the spot where the lynching happened. I combed through records online and visited the local history museum. The incident was well-known to local historians, but there were no monuments or memorials. In fact, as we put together the pieces of geography we realized that the bridge where the lynching had taken place was no longer in existence. Instead, the marshland had dried up and become firm ground. The lynching spot was now a road next to the one high school in town, in between two sports fields.

My husband had built a white cross that we had put in the trunk of our car, and we wrote down the name of the man who was killed decades before our own parents were alive: Alonzo Tucker. We tried to hammer the cross into the ground, to make a small, permanent, and stubborn marker of remembrance. I envisioned high schoolers on their way to track practice taking pictures and googling the name, learning the history they were walking past. But the gravel was hard and we didn't have proper tools. We leaned the cross against the chain-link fence, said a prayer and left, spooked by the police cars patrolling the area. Had we done something wrong? I wondered. Had we broken some sort of law? I don't think we did, but for some reason it felt like trying to make a memorial to a victim of White supremacy was a transgression of sorts. The first rule of empire is that you never, ever expose the ways it retains its power.

The threads of this narrative reach everywhere, into every state in our country. As Soong-Chan Rah suggests, we need to get to the larger narrative or nothing will change. White supremacy is a foundational element of the myth of the American Dream—it is a belief that has been internalized and absorbed, passed down by the European conquerors and how they tried to make sense of their world. Without addressing this larger narrative, structures that oppress will continue to pop up: slavery gets changed into Jim Crow laws, which get changed into the mass incarceration system (indeed, there are now more Black men in the US prison system than were a part of slavery).

It's the same reason why Bryan Stevenson eventually transitioned his career from working to exonerate wrongly accused Black men on death row to trying to change the larger narratives in America. His most recent project, the monument and memorial to peace and justice in Montgomery, is the first ever monument to America's history of lynching. As Stevenson is fond of pointing out, it took only a decade for there to be a monument to the victims of 9/11. Why has it taken our country so long to mourn other tragedies, to lament the loss of life and violence inflicted on so many within our nation?

Perhaps it's because up till now the monuments and memorials have not been made for or by exiles. Instead, they've been placed by people in power, by people who have a lot to gain by upholding the way things have always worked. Empire loves to create statues to itself—think of the bull on Wall Street, the statues of Confederate leaders littering public parks in the South, the four men carved into Mt. Rushmore. They all keep the narrative intact. But as writer

Ta-Nehisi Coates says in regard to the history of racialized violence in this country—including 250 years of slavery, ninety years of Jim Crow, sixty years of separate but equal, and thirty-five years of racist housing policies: "Until we reckon with our compounding moral debts, America will never be whole."[4]

The day I made a pilgrimage to the site of Alonzo Tucker's lynching was one step in a journey toward learning how to lament. I was starting to pay attention to those bodies that have been crucified here in my own country, those bodies that most closely resemble Christ's own body. We will never be liberated until the true exiles are the ones making the memorials, the monuments, the songs we sing, until the systems are dismantled that have worked for me but imprisoned others.

Growing up, I was prepared to be persecuted; I was prepared to be labeled a freak, an outsider. I was prepared to be a proud exile, certain of my outsider status. But I was not prepared for the opposite: to learn to how to mourn the systems and sins of my community, to learn how to live as a member of a society that benefits from unjust systems. In arenas packed with people, in the halls of government buildings, in churches large and small, in universities and conferences, I was not taught to learn how to lay down my power willingly. I was taught to fight for it, which dulled and tarnished my ability to mourn the reality of those who truly were being oppressed in my midst. And if I can't learn to lament and repent, I will never be able to envision a world where resurrection is truly possible.

25 ★ LEARNING FROM EXILES

I ONCE HAD THE GOOD FORTUNE to see a touring production of *Hamilton* for my birthday, thanks to my brother-in-law. When the day came, I woke up with a fever, plugged sinuses, a miserable headache. A head cold to end all head colds, perhaps the worst of my life—but I couldn't not go. I watched as gorgeous men and women of all shapes and colors reenacted a history that was profound and relevant and revisionist in a way that called us to a better future. When it came to the part where George Washington sang the song "One Last Time" about the radical act of abdicating power and responsibility in order to invite others to do the same, I couldn't stop sobbing.

Lin-Manuel Miranda, creator of the musical, has Washington sing one of our Founding Father's supposedly favorite Bible verses: "Everyone shall sit under their own vine, and fig tree, and no one shall make them afraid, they will be safe in this nation we've made." It's a reference to Micah 4:4, which also speaks about the nations beating their swords into ploughshares, about there being no more war when God is the judge. When the actor who plays George Washington sang those lines, it was as if my own heart was being laid bare, and I couldn't stop crying. This dream was my dream too.

As I sobbed at *Hamilton*, I felt a homesickness for a world I had never fully experienced. Was I having a spiritual moment, or did I just have a wicked fever? I don't know, exactly, but this is why, for me, the word *joy* does not adequately describe how I feel when I catch glimpses of God's dream for the world. C. S. Lewis described this feeling with the German word *sehnsucht*, which means a longing, wistful nostalgia, which he sometimes called Beauty.[1] In *The Weight of Glory*, Lewis writes,

> These things—the beauty, the memory of our own past—are good images of what we really desire; but if they are mistaken for the thing itself they turn into dumb idols, breaking the hearts of their worshipers. For they are not the thing itself; they are only the scent of a flower we have not found, the echo of a tune we have not heard, news from a country we have never yet visited.[2]

What Lewis calls beauty and I sometimes call "longing for another world" is translated *shalom* in the Bible. In the Hebrew Scriptures the word *shalom* is used 550 times, and it connotes a combination of well-being, wholeness, the perfection of God's creation, abundance, and peace. And as theologian Lisa Sharon Harper writes in *The Very Good Gospel*, it shows how the individual is connected to the larger system. "The peace of self is dependent on the peace of the other. God created the world in a web of relationships that overflowed with forceful goodness."[3]

Harper looks at the beginning of the Bible, the story of creation. There God's creation was imbued with inherent goodness between the living creatures, the land, and humanity. This is where our dream starts, and it was given by God. Even though the nightmares crop up frequently—the Bible is full of stories so horrible they make my teeth ache—the dream keeps cropping up. Shalom still pops up over and over again—from the Garden of Eden to the Sabbath laws to the prophets and their declarations of God's Holy Mountain and the Day of the Lord.[4] There are the Jubilee laws about freeing those in debt and bondage every fifty years and letting fields lie fallow every seven. There is the manna in the wilderness and an economy that rejects the immorality of both extreme poverty and extreme wealth. There are the Ten Commandments, the antithesis of Pharaoh, who made the empire god and exploited his neighbors for the sake of progress. There are all the places God admonished the people to care for the vulnerable, the orphan, the widow, and the foreigner. And there is the persistent refrain that God's dream for the world will always come hand in hand with justice: that without justice there will always be neighbors who go unloved, who are exploited, who are forgotten in our quest for affluence, autonomy, safety, and power.

★ ★ ★

Exiles point out where shalom is not being experienced in our world—both currently and in our pasts. As I continue to study history, the story of Ida B. Wells, the famed antilynching crusader, leaps out of the pages for me. Ida lived through the Reconstruction era in the 1860s and 1870s. It was a time when freed Black men and women began to hold more political, social, and economic power for the first time, pushing the limits of the rhetoric of democracy so freely espoused and yet rarely enacted for all. And then came the backlash, the post-Reconstruction era, when the White establishment responded with various forms of racial terror. One of the ways this happened was the enactment of Jim Crow laws decades after slavery was abolished. Another was public lynchings—Black men, women, and children were killed without trial for supposed crimes, a violent visual means to inspire terror and subjugation while consolidating power in the hands of the White perpetrators.

Ida was angry watching her rights stripped away through Jim Crow, and when three men she knew personally were lynched on the outskirts of Memphis, Tennessee, she wrote an editorial lambasting the injustice she saw. Ida crisply pointed out that eight Negroes had been lynched since the last issue of the paper had gone out,

> three for killing a white man, and five on the same old racket—the new alarm about raping white women. The same program of hanging, then shooting bullets into the lifeless bodies was carried out to the letter. Nobody in this section of the country believes in that threadbare lie that Negro men rape white women. If Southern Men are not careful, they will overreach themselves and public sentiment will have a reaction.[5]

Ida dared to publicly call out the myth used to justify lynchings—that all Black men were violent, especially toward White women. That editorial changed the course of Wells's life. The same day it went to print, the same Southern men she had named in her piece—White newspaper editors—called for her to be publicly killed and mutilated (in a horrible twist, even as they advocated for violence against her, they still somehow found a way to congratulate themselves on their Southern respectability at holding off as long as they did). Wells was forced to flee Memphis, and the newspaper office she co-owned was ransacked and destroyed by mobs; her fellow Black journalists barely escaped with their lives. In a statement about the ordeal, Ida signed her name as "Exiled"—this was her new reality. She didn't return to Memphis for thirty years. She was exiled from her home because she wrote the truth when no one else would. In her case the truth was a question: if this isn't really about Black men raping White women, then what is it about? It was about strategic, vigilante terrorism aimed at suppressing an entire race, carried out in public without any consequences.

Wells wrote that she was exiled from her home for merely "hinting at the truth" that public lynchings were one step in a concrete effort to terrorize Black people and take away their rights in a post–Civil War America. The truth she was hinting at was the pervasiveness of White supremacy at work, which led to Jim Crow laws, housing segregation, unequal and segregated education, and eventually soaring mass-incarceration rates. All legal, respectable ways of dehumanizing and criminalizing an entire race of people. Wells, along with so many others who have chipped away at the lies and the myths that surround us—declaring that only some people are our neighbors, that only some people deserve power and privilege and God's blessing—their hintings have become a street lamp to light my path, at great cost to themselves.

The suffering of exiles like Ida B. Wells—and Larnell Bruce Jr., Dr. Martin Luther King Jr., Malcolm X, Alonzo Tucker, and John Perkins, among many others—ties us to the Christian story of a God who came to earth and suffered with humanity. Theologian James

Cone writes that in the lynching era, 1880–1940, "White Christians lynched nearly five thousand black men and women in a manner with obvious echoes to Roman crucifixion of Jesus."[6] But the Christians perpetrating this violence didn't notice the similarity between the cross of the Lord they worshiped and the crosses they created out of lynching trees. For decades, Western theologians were unable to see Jesus in the bodies that swayed from those trees, the victims who were killed to satisfy the fear of the masses. This omission, this obvious and terrifying lack of understanding haunts me. I myself did not and could not see the connections between people experiencing racial terror in my own country and the Suffering Servant I claimed to follow. I couldn't see it, that is, until exiles in the landscape of the American Dream pointed it out to me.

George Washington referred to the beautiful dream of Micah 4:4 over fifty times during the course of his life.[7] The irony of this should not escape us. This country's first president owned hundreds of slaves. He created a mythology around his teeth (he claimed they were wooden, just like the cherry tree he supposedly chopped down and refused to lie about) in order to cover up the truth: he had the teeth of slaves arranged for his own macabre dentures. He was a president, who, like most of his peers, justified a practice he knew to be wrong—the enslavement and dehumanization of an entire race of people—to promote the success of certain kinds of people in America. Freedom, liberty, and justice for all: he wrote and spoke about these values, even as he used his power to deny these values to enslaved people on his property. He spoke of longing for a world where everyone flourished, where each person had their own vine and fig tree, yet all the while he built his own plantation—his own American Dream—on the backs of broken families and broken cultures. He wrote with bright hope for America's future, even as he stole hope from those he enslaved.

I want to be careful when I talk about shalom. There is a long and storied history of people working to ensure the flourishing of only a few and calling it good news. Indigenous author and theologian Randy Woodley calls the kingdom of God the community of creation, reminding me of this connection to true shalom, to Eden as it was before we were exiled. But it doesn't stop there. The only way to learn to both identify our longing for and live into shalom is by being in relationship to those who are the most affected by broken systems and broken relationships. Exiles, or the stranger or the foreigner, are a part of the triad of the vulnerable—including widows and orphans—that the Scriptures constantly tell the people of God to care for. Why is that? Woodley says a consistent standard is given through the Bible: "Shalom is always tested on the margins of society and revealed by how the poor, oppressed, disempowered, and needy are treated." Much of the Bible is concerned with wealth and economics, pointing out how a huge gap between the wealthy and the poor is an indicator of the lack of shalom in a society, and Woodley writes that these wealth discrepancies both then and now lead to all sorts of societal ills—including injustice, false imprisonment, unemployment, homelessness, hunger, and more.[8] He also says that God has a special concern for the poor and needy, "because how we treat them reveals our hearts, regardless of the rhetoric we employ to make ourselves sound just."

There is a reason I cried at *Hamilton*. I wanted to believe that my country really was a place where all kinds of people could flourish. I cried because I want to live in a world where Micah 4:4 comes true, and I cried because I don't, not right now. I cried because I live in a country full of Christians where there are also camps full of migrant children being held at the border, separated from their families. It's a country where there is little popular incentive to create legal pathways for citizenship for the majority of people seeking economic opportunities or freedom. It's a country that encourages excess consumption and consumerism paid for by the exploitation of others, a country that refuses to acknowledge its past sins and so repeats them. At some point the Christians who live in this country have to decide: Are we okay with the way our world works? Or do we long to see a different dream start to grow?

Part of the work of listening to exiles means putting down our knee-jerk reaction to only highlight the good, the revisionist histories that only amplify the parts we want to keep. For people who come from a dominant culture background or multiple variations—someone like myself, who is White, American, and Christian—it can often feel overwhelming. Do we need to dismantle everything? How can we fix it quickly? And how in the actual world are we supposed to move forward? I acknowledge that some readers might be experiencing these feelings right now because I myself contain those questions within me. But as someone who came from power and was raised to seek out power, the truth is that I cannot and will not answer any of these questions. I sit in my loss, in my blindness. I sit in the loneliness of watching my carefully constructed theologies and ideologies crumble as I listen to the stories of those who have been wounded along the road. I sit in the wide, wide shadow of the dream that people like George Washington had for my country. I practice the discipline of cultivating the tenacious hope of a world where no one is ever made afraid, where everyone has a vine and fig tree, a place to live and a place of meaningful work and dignity.

This dream is not yet a reality, and at times I despair of truly ever seeing glimpses of shalom in the land of the living. The only ones who can help us inch toward this new kind of world are those who have never felt safe, who have never had access to all that I who have taken for granted. The only way we will ever start to see the kingdom of God come to earth is by following the lead of the true exiles among us.

EPILOGUE ✶ HOW TO LIVE IN EMPIRE

I REMEMBER RECENTLY LEARNING about the Beguines, thirteenth-century female Christian mystics who started their own religious order after being denied access to worship God anywhere else. They were holy fools who were committed to paying attention in a society obsessed with hierarchy and economy. Writer Jesse van Eerdman says that these women were like newborn puppies with their eyes licked open by God.[1] What a glorious thought: God is the one who opens us up to the blurry world with maternal devotion and a desire to see us truly, fully alive. These women looked very hard at the hand God had given them—a world full of suffering and crusades and wars, a world where, as single or widowed women, they were not valued in their society—and they found a good king and a good kingdom, one defined by love and service; God was present everywhere they looked.

I am less a holy fool and more of an angst-ridden harbinger of doom, but I see the roots of love beginning to bloom in some rather strange places in my life. Waking up to the world has not felt like my eyes have been licked open so much as I have been forced to face realities I would rather pretend don't exist: injustice and inequality and unrighteousness at every turn. But as I cultivate my eyes to see the bad, I also work toward that discipline of delight, of paying attention to the scent of shalom when I experience it. Recently I realized one of my happiest moments is when I am in our local elementary school cafeteria, the smell of broccoli lingering in my nose. When there are women everywhere scattered like seeds along the long tables for another Friday English class. It's as orderly as a garden overgrown in late summer—people huddled in clusters of threes and fours, some people tutoring while other people practice.

I'm the happiest seeing the connections being made all around me. People getting what they need, people helping each other in mutual ways: "Here's the best halal meat market." "Here is how to find a good interpreter." "Here is how I talked to my landlord about my problem." I stand in the corner of the cafeteria, usually double-checking to make sure I've marked everyone present, eyeballing to make sure the tutors don't need more worksheets, figuring out whether now is a good time to make coffee and then serving it to everyone. Everything is slightly chaotic, but there are so many smiles that I stand in the corner, grinning like an idiot, a lightness on my shoulders as we slip into a place of blessing that transcends any ethic of hierarchy—where all, instead of a few, are seen as teachers.

My joy comes from a desire that is not born in me but comes from the Creator God—the desire to see children, women, and men be known as beloved. The community English class every Friday in our elementary school cafeteria smells of belovedness as much as of vegetables and pizza sauce, because it's a space designed for everyone to flourish, not just a few. Spaces like these are increasingly rare in a capitalized, privatized society, which is why it sticks out when I see it. It feels like a shelter from the outside storm; it feels like a place where together we can start to build our own sort of society, to piece together a nest built out of mutuality, stories, laughter, and sorrow. A place to learn to blink our eyes, to see the image of God sitting right next to us in disguises that might continue to surprise us.

★ ★ ★

I started this book by looking at the way Jesus announced his ministry: he was bringing good news to the poor, the captive, the blind, the oppressed, and to proclaim the year of the Lord's favor. I wanted to examine the opposite values—affluence, autonomy, safety, and power—and to pay attention to how strong they are in my life and in the larger narrative of the American experiment.

I purposefully left off a portion of that announcement in Luke 4, just as Jesus did in that synagogue so many years ago. His original audience must have been familiar with Isaiah, and they would have eagerly been waiting for the conclusion to that grand list of proclamations toward the poor and disposed—In Isaiah 61 it says, "to proclaim the year of the Lord's favor, and the day of vengeance of our God." God was on the side of Israel, after all, in the face of large and terrible empires like Egypt, Assyria, Babylon, and then Rome, and vengeance was a divinely ordained right of the oppressed. But Jesus leaves them hanging; he leaves them without that last line. Jesus leaves out the part about vengeance, and for a moment the crowd is still with him even as he sits down with a flourish and says, "Today this Scripture has been fulfilled in your hearing." In fact, they "all spoke well of him, and marveled."

But in the space of a few verses, everything changes. Jesus goes on to give two examples of people in the Hebrew Scriptures who God blessed and worked through—the widow of Zarephath, and Naaman the Syrian. Jesus points out that there must have been other widows in need of sustenance, but God chose to provide for a faithful Gentile. There were many people with leprosy who longed to be healed, he says, but God chose a Gentile again—and a powerful one who seems to subvert the very values that Jesus has just said are high on his priority list. In a second the mood changes and the crowd rushes to murder Jesus by driving him out of the temple and attempting to throw him off a cliff. It's the first attempt on Jesus' life, one that we don't talk about as much. It is a foreshadowing of the crucifixion.

What made the crowd so angry? It's the most challenging, radical message of all: God is indeed rescuing, loving, and moving in the very communities that we would most like to exclude from the good news. Jesus wasn't attacked for speaking the truth about a God who demands sacrifice and obedience, who is only working out God's plan through a specific, chosen people. The crowd rushed and tried to kill Jesus for saying the opposite, for leaving out the bits about judgment against perceived enemies and for saying the kingdom would come from those we were taught to hate and despise. That God was not just on the side of the chosen few but had swung wide the gates of love.

Jesus and his announcement of what he came to do in the world enraged those who had been taught they were the *chosen people*. If we are not careful, our own hearts can be twisted to feel the same anger and fear as we lose our spot as the pinnacle of God's creation in our own minds or our societies. I see parallels of this in my own story: as a missionary in training, as a White evangelical Christian, as a teacher, I am forever grappling with the legacy of rightness, of supremacy, of placing myself at the center of Jesus' work in the world when I was always supposed to be somewhere on the edges. I am constantly challenged by where I have seen Jesus and where I have experienced shalom. And I know I am not alone. Jesus attracted all kinds of people. He was, and remains, good news even for those who have benefited from the systems of the world—if only we have the eyes to see it.

★ ★ ★

The first person who astonished Jesus in the book of Luke was in fact a higher-up in the Roman government, part of the empire that was oppressing the people of God. A few chapters after his pronouncement Jesus was asked by a centurion—a man in charge of hundreds of soldiers—to heal his very sick servant via messengers. When Jesus is on his way the centurion sends a curious message:

> Lord, do not trouble yourself, for I am not worthy to have you come under my roof; therefore I did not presume to come to you. But only speak the word, and let my servant be healed. For I also am a man set under authority, with soldiers under me; and I say to one, "Go," and he goes, and to another, "Come," and he comes, and to my slave, "Do this," and the slave does it.

Luke then tells us that Jesus was amazed at the centurion, and turning to the crowd that followed him he said, "'I tell you, not even in Israel have I found such faith.' And when those who had been sent returned to the house, they found the slave in good health" (Luke 7:1-10).

The centurion didn't fit any of the categories in Luke 4. He wasn't the target audience for Jesus' ministry. So how did he recognize and believe who Jesus was and what Jesus came to do more than anyone else at this point in the Gospels? I think the key is his relationship with his servant, the one he asks Jesus to heal. I think the centurion was transformed not just by his proximity to his slave but by the experience of entering into his suffering. He was able to see Jesus for who he was because he was in relationship with someone who desperately needed good news, who needed shalom. This ultimately is what allowed him to experience the liberating presence of Jesus.

People love to say that proximity will fix everything. All we have to do is live next door to each other, they say, and our problems will melt away as we gather together for block parties or dinners over long tables. But this isn't true. My own neighborhood is a perfect example of this, as are so many of our cities. Living side by side with one another can even make a situation worse: when the oppressed and oppressor are locked in a dance to keep one subservient and the other in power, anger and violence (both physical and ideological) are inevitable. Proximity plus toxic narratives and unequal power lead to more oppression.

This is where the Christian story transcends the easy platitudes of neoliberalism or cultural relativism. It reminds us that something else is needed beyond thoughts and prayers or good intentions. Moving into underresourced neighborhoods or sending our kids to the same schools or eating at the same table with people who have experienced marginalization isn't enough (although those can be good first steps). Proximity only changes us if we enter into other peoples' suffering. Only when we allow ourselves to experience the bad news of their world, without rushing to explain it away. Only when we take on the suffering of other people to the point that we will do whatever we can to make it right, even if it includes losing some of our own money, rights, safety, and power.

★ ★ ★

Sometimes this upside-down world of the kingdom of God looks like dismantling systems, creatively subverting them, or simply protesting them with whatever resources available to us. Sometimes it looks like moving somewhere else, voluntarily giving up positions of power, or learning to check the impulse to hoard resources for ourselves or our families. And sometimes it looks like leaning into the simple pleasures of a life lived in interconnectedness, imitating the resilient joy of our neighbors who have experienced exile.

I'm a little bit obsessed with an idea coined by theologian Kelley Nikondeha—what she calls "relational reparations." The kingdom of God, Nikondeha says, comes when the people of God give back to those the empire has stolen from. The hallmark of stories of relational reparations is its wonderful creativity—seen throughout Scriptures (the story of Bithiah and Miriam, of the centurion soldier, of Zacchaeus) and in our own world as well. This is where the Christian witness will continue on, long after empires or political and economic power shifts. It will be in the stories of people coming together to follow Jesus, the privileged giving up what they have to enter into real relationship with their new family, their brothers and sisters in Christ.

A friend told me a story about a man in her mission organization. This man—let's call him Carl—lived and worked in a low-income community that was mostly Spanish speaking. People were often sent to court for minor infractions like running a red light, and many of them faced steep fines and even jail time. Carl decided that he was going to start showing up with his friends when they were called to court. A tall White man, he would dress in a suit and bring a briefcase with him. He would say nothing at all; just his presence was enough for his friends' cases to be dropped, dismissed, or the fines lowered. Carl knew he couldn't overturn the entire criminal justice system—he couldn't change how the system heavily policed the poor and discriminated against Black and Brown youth—all on his own. So he decided to work the system in his own way. Whenever he and his friends would leave court, Carl would open his briefcase and reveal what was inside: a bag of Doritos, which they would eat with relish.

I know people who buy duplexes in poor neighborhoods. They live in one half of the duplex with their family and rent the other at rates well below the market. I know other people who routinely give up speaking gigs to people who aren't usually given a platform in such places—primarily women and people of color. I know other people who spend a year reading only books by people of color and who find in the process that it's a delight to be immersed in new worlds of thought and scholarship. I know people who commit to listening and learning from theologies and voices they don't always agree with, committing themselves to the discipline of being quiet and listening to another perspective. All of these people find they are changing, shifting, as their worlds expand outward. It looks a lot like the joy of welcoming a new baby into the family—the gift of the unexpected, the birth of new possibilities.

There's the librarian who sings the name of each child at the weekly story time, a silly little song that repeats the name of the child over and over again and makes the children all beam with happiness. He tells me he sings this song not just as a way to learn their names but as a way to combat the negativity they might hear in their own life. He tells me studies show that saying a child's name in a positive tone eight times a day can help undo the damage of only hearing their name when they're in trouble for something. I think about this, about a man in a small library's multipurpose room, singing and clapping and saying each child's name with love and joy, his own little ministry of naming.

I know people who are creative in the ways they love the planet, finding great joy in reusing, repurposing, and doing without. They do this with love, not from a sense of deprivation or duty—like my friend Leah, who came to me breathless with excitement one day because she had discovered how to cook a pot of beans while using the lowest amount of energy. "You just take a pot full of beans and water, put a lid on it, boil on the stove for ten minutes, then wrap the pot with a bunch of blankets and stick it in a suitcase for twelve hours—then viola! You have a perfect pot of beans!" Would I ever be so pleased about something as simple (or not so simple) as figuring out how to conserve energy for fun?

I have friends who honor a creative God by using their own imaginative energies to make paintings, quilts, books, podcasts, songs, stamps—anything that brings beauty to the world, anything that is worth creating in a world obsessed with consumption. Friends who cook the meals their mothers made and friends who try new and exotic (to them) spices and tastes—all of them modeling what it means to feast in the house of the Lord. People who make casseroles for single mothers struggling to keep up. Businesswomen (like my sister Lindsay) who routinely donate their time and energies to help underresourced communities access information that will help their livelihoods. People like my other sister, Candyce, who throw themselves into learning little-known languages, all the better to make certain people feel slightly more at home in the world.

I have friends who always have somebody living with them like it's no big deal. Friends who feel responsibility for their neighbors, even if they just met them on the side of the road. Friends who turn a chance encounter into a lifelong friendship. Friends who reject the isolation and autonomy of the surrounding culture and find creative ways to cram more people, more life, and more love into their spaces. Friends who coax gardens out of places that used to be deserts and who let their plants go to seed to feed the birds and the bees, looking for the kingdom to come even in the smallest of ways.

★ ★ ★

Walter Brueggemann writes that "poets have no advice to give people. They only want people to see differently, to re-vision life. They are not coercive. They only try to stimulate, hint, give nuance, not more. They cannot do more, because they are making available a world that does not yet exist beyond their imagination."[2] My heart leaps within me when I read this. In the end I want to be a poet more than I want to be a prophet: someone who pays attention and sees the world and yet has the imagination and audacity to envision a different future.

A few years ago I got a tattoo on my arm. It's of a tree, its branches spread out, a few birds in its branches. At the base of the trunk is a tiny seed. It's a mustard seed, the symbol of faith in Jesus' parable of a mustard seed (Mark 4:30-32). The mustard seed is the smallest of all seeds, but it grows up to be a tall tree, where the birds of the air can make their home.

Once we get a taste of the goodness of Jesus, we won't ever want to go back to the old dreams, the ones that didn't have space for all the birds of the air to make their home. This new dream starts with a seed, but it ends with a tree of life, with room for all the birds of the air to make their nests. I tattooed this parable on my body because I know how easy it is to give in to the values of my culture. It reminds me to keep listening, keep lamenting, keep pointing my eyes toward the edges. When I see peace and joy and flourishing for my neighbors who have suffered so much, then I experience it myself. I hold this dream close to my heart, as tiny as the smallest seed.

When I walk around my neighborhood, I see the moss and the litter, I see the school full of joy and economic neglect, and I see neighbors forging a way forward in the shadow of loss and lack of power and dependence on each other. I see the kingdom of God coming up through the cracks in the neighborhoods many of us were taught to ignore and in the voices of those who have long been pushed to the margins. I see a tree growing strong and safe and big enough for us all to find shelter and an imagination forming that's not dependent on old ways of thinking about economics, privacy, safety, individualism, or power. I see a large tree growing ever taller; I see myself caught safely in its branches.

In the end we will not go back to a garden, a solitary experience with God. Instead, the kingdom coming will look like a new city, full to bursting with people—just like the apartments here at the edge of our city. For now I am like a bird myself, a magpie for the Lord seeking out the small seeds of shalom being planted here and now, eager for the day when they will burst forth. One day I will find my shelter, my true home with all the other beloved birds of the air.

ACKNOWLEDGMENTS

THIS BOOK IS THE PRODUCT OF YEARS of thoughts tumbling around my head, and now they are in a book you are reading. I still can't believe it. I could not have done this without the support of my person, the best boy, Krispin. You are full of tireless empathy and kindness; you soften all my extremely sharp edges. I love you. To my children, Ramona and Ransom: you teach me about the kingdom of God every day, and when I grow up I hope I am more like you: full of anger at injustice, full of wonder and hope that the world could be a different way. Also I hope I can learn to dance like you.

To my writing group and our endless hours of conversation, laughter, and solidarity: Amy Peterson, Stina Kielsmeier-Cook, Jessica Goudeau, Christiana Peterson: I couldn't do this without you. Special thanks to Kelley Nikondeha, who is both my personal cheerleader and my very favorite theologian, who stirs up the flame of love within me for a very good God. To my Tuesday night prayer group and all the lovely souls who have been a part of it for the past four years: thank you for helping me learn to give the burdens of my community back to God.

This book is indebted to the work of Adam McInturf at Windows Booksellers, who is the very best reference librarian friend a gal could ever have. I am especially thankful for the careful reading and editing of Breanna Randall, who from half the world away gently pointed out so many of my blind spots. To the Newbigin House of Studies and the many amazing conversations I had in your program, I am forever grateful. Special thanks for the rich conversations and learning I experienced with Dr. Peter Choi, Julie Rodgers, Mira Joyner, and Sally Steele. To the Collegeville Institute and the amazing work they do to support writers of faith: thank you. To the people who encouraged me, supported me, let me stay in their houses while I toiled away on this in the margins of my life, thank you. Harriet Congdon, Shawn Strannigan (hi Mom!), Lindsay Strannigan and Candyce Wani (hi sisters!), Brittany Win Lee, Josina Guess, Shannan Martin, and Becca Stanley. You all make me feel less lonely in the world.

I am thankful to everyone who gives me and my intense little heart the chance to publish, including my agent Rachelle Gardner, my editor Ethan McCarthy, and the good folks at InterVarsity Press.

To my neighbors, I am at a loss for words. To say thank you for the ways you have shaped me, quieted me, pressed me to speak up seems entirely inadequate. You have revealed to me the pharaoh that lies within my bones, you have shown me both how awful the world is and how much God sees and loves us all anyway. You make my heart burn and my brain never stop spinning. You most likely will never read this acknowledgment but I have to say it anyway: thank you for showing me the way forward every single day.

NOTES

Introduction

[1]See chapter 4, "Color Blind," of Michael O. Emerson and Christian Smith, *Divided by Faith: Evangelical Religion and the Problem of Race in America* (New York: Oxford University Press, 2000).

[2]"When sin is limited to the individual realm and does not extend into the corporate realm, our understanding of salvation is also limited to the individual realm." Soong-Chan Rah, *The Next Evangelicalism: Releasing the Church from Western Cultural Captivity* (Downers Grove, IL: InterVarsity Press, 2012), 40.

[3]Hafiz and Daniel James Ladinsky, *The Gift: Poems by the Great Sufi Master* (New York: Arkana, 1999), 300.

1. The Walls of Rome

[1]Richard Horsley, foreword to Walter Brueggemann, *Money and Possessions* (Louisville, KY: Westminster John Knox, 2016), xii.

[2]John Dominic Crossan, "Roman Imperial Theology," in *In the Shadow of Empire: Reclaiming the Bible as a History of Faithful Resistance* Richard A. Horsley, ed., (Louisville, KY: Westminster John Knox, 2008), 73.

2. Who Is My Neighbor?

[1]Rachel Sherman, *Uneasy Street: The Anxieties of Affluence* (Princeton, NJ: Princeton University Press, 2019).

[2]Martin Luther King Jr., *Strength to Love* (Minneapolis: Fortress Press, 2010), 69.

[3]See William T. Cavanaugh, "Attachment and Detachment," in *Being Consumed: Economics and Christian Desire* (Grand Rapids, MI: Eerdmans, 2009).

[4]King, *Strength to Love*, 68.

3. Getting Curious

[1]"Mapping Inequality: Redlining in New Deal America," Digital Scholarship Lab, accessed August 3, 2019, https://dsl.richmond.edu/panorama/redlining.

[2]Greg Nokes, "Black Exclusion Laws in Oregon," *Oregon Encyclopedia*, accessed September 17, 2019, https://oregonencyclopedia.org/articles/exclusion_laws/#.XUS_Z5NKi5w.

[3]"1970-2017: The Depressing Decline in Black Home Ownership Rates in Oregon and City of Portland," *Oregon Housing Blog*, January 23, 2019, http://oregon housing.blogspot.com/2019/01/1970-2017-depressing-decline-in-black.html.

[4]Óscar A. Romero and Carolyn Kurtz, *The Scandal of Redemption: When God Liberates the Poor, Saves Sinners, and Heals Nations* (Walden, NY: Plough, 2018), 21.

[5]Martin Luther King Jr., *Strength to Love* (Minneapolis: Fortress Press, 2010), 37.

[6]Jonathan Wilson-Hargrove, *Reconstructing the Gospel: Finding Freedom from Slaveholder Religion* (Downers Grove, IL: InterVarsity Press, 2018).

[7]Stephanie Dickrell, "Nearly 74,000 Speak at Least Some Somali in Minnesota," *SCTimes*, October 22, 2017, www.sctimes.com/story/news/local/2017/10/22/nearly-74-000-speak-least-some-somali-minnesota/783691001/https://multco.us/file/56387/download.

[8]Meizhu Lui et al., *The Color of Wealth: The Story Behind the US Racial Wealth Divide* (New York: New Press, 2006), 8.

[9]I recommend doing a deep dive on redlining in your specific city; everyone, however, can read Thomas Sugrue, *The Origins of the Urban Crisis: Race and Inequality in Postwar Detroit* (Princeton, NJ: Princeton University Press, 2005).

[10]Read her book: Julia Dinsmore, *My Name Is Child of God . . . Not "Those People"* (Minneapolis: Augsburg Fortress, 2007).

4. Low, Low Prices

[1]Read Karen Gonzales, *The God Who Sees* (Harrisonburg, VA: Herald Press, 2019). See also Phyllis Trible and Letty M. Russel, eds., *Hagar, Sarah, and Their Children* (Louisville, KY: Westminster John Knox, 2006).

[2]Melissa Florer-Bixler, email interview, August 4, 2019. The story is taken from the Babylonian Talmud, *Yoma* 76a.

[3]Walter Brueggemann, *Money and Possessions* (Louisville, KY: Westminster John Knox, 2016), 17.

[4]William T. Cavanaugh, *Being Consumed: Economics and Christian Desire* (Grand Rapids, MI: Eerdmans, 2009), 94.

[5]Liz Theoharis, *Always with Us? What Jesus Really Said About the Poor* (Grand Rapids, MI: Eerdmans, 2017), 10-11.

[6]Find these and the following statistics in Ronald J. Sider, "Crucial Economic Data," in *Fixing the Moral Deficit: A Balanced Way to Balance the Budget* (Downers Grove, IL: InterVarsity Press, 2012).

[7]Sider, *Fixing the Moral Deficit*, 29.

[8]Cavanaugh, *Being Consumed*, 91.

5. How Not to Be a Millionaire

[1]"Lazarus at the Gate: An Economic Discipleship Guide," Boston Faith and Justice Network, 2012, www.theologyofwork.org/uploads/general/lazarus-at-the-gate-curriculum.pdf.

[2]Dorothy Day and Robert Ellsberg, *The Duty of Delight: The Diaries of Dorothy Day* (New York: Image Books, 2011).

[3]Dorothy Day, "Love Is the Measure," *Catholic Worker*, June 2, 1946, www.catholicworker.org/dorothyday/articles/425.html.

[4]Day, "Love Is the Measure."

6. Lament for the Land

[1]Peter Moskowitz, *How to Kill a City: Gentrification, Inequality, and the Fight for the Neighborhood* (New York: Nation Books, 2018), 57.

[2]Lisa Sharon Harper, *The Very Good Gospel* (Colorado Springs, CO: WaterBrook, 2016), 14.

7. True Generosity

[1]Robin Wall Kimmerer, *Braiding Sweetgrass: Indigenous Wisdom, Scientific Knowledge and the Teachings of Plants* (Minneapolis: Milkweed, 2013), 108.

[2]Kimmerer, *Braiding Sweetgrass*, 115.

[3]Kimmerer, *Braiding Sweetgrass*, 114.

10. Fresh Paint

[1]Nikole Hannah Jones, "Choosing a School for My Daughter in a Segregated City," *New York Times*, June 9, 2016, www.nytimes.com/2016/06/12/magazine/choosing-a-school-for-my-daughter-in-a-segregated-city.html.

[2]"Overview and Mission Statement," US Department of Education, accessed September 18, 2019, www2.ed.gov/about/landing.jhtml.

11. What Is Education For?

[1]Maxwell King, *The Good Neighbor: The Life and Work of Fred Rogers* (New York: Abrams Press, 2019), 251.

[2]Alexis Ditkowsky, "The Children We Mean to Raise: The Real Messages Adults Are Sending About Values," Making Caring Common Project, July 7, 2014, https://mcc.gse.harvard.edu/reports/children-mean-raise.

13. The Hospitality of Exiles

[1]Thomas Merton, *Conjectures of a Guilty Bystander* (New York: Image Books, 1968), 155.

14. The Odds

[1]"Odds of Dying," National Safety Council, accessed August 11, 2019, https://injuryfacts.nsc.org/all-injuries/preventable-death-overview/odds-of-dying.

[2]Padraig O'Tuama, from a lecture given at the Festival of Faith and Writing. For more of Padraig's work, check out his poetry collections and his book of non-fiction called *In the Shelter* (London: Hodder Faith, 2015).

[3]Alex Nowrasteh, "Terrorism and Immigration: Risk Factors," *Policy Analysis* 798 (September 2016).

15. Mary, or, We Can Never Be Safe

[1]Eula Biss, *On Immunity: An Inoculation* (Minneapolis: Milkweed Press, 2014).

16. The Ship of the Doomed

[1]Approximately half of this chapter is lightly adapted from D. L. Mayfield, "Feasting in the House of the Lord," *Curator*, October 22, 2018, www.curatormagazine.com/d-l-mayfield/23426.

[2]For more information on the Rohingya crisis, see "Rohingya Refugee Crisis," OCHA, accessed September 19, 2019, www.unocha.org/rohingya-refugee-crisis.

[3]Jessica Goudeau, *After the Last Border* (New York: Viking, 2020).

17. Good Seeds

[1]Now I tend to agree with missiologist Lesslie Newbigin that Matthew 28 is one of three great commissions given in Scripture, along with John 20 and Luke 4.

[2]There are many places to look up these numbers, but I rely heavily on the work of Jenny Yang and Matthew Soerens, both of World Relief. See Matthew Soerens and Jenny Yang, "Soerens and Yang: Trump Has a Choice to Make—Ban Refugees or Truly Restore American Greatness?" *Fox News*, July 27, 2019, www.foxnews.com/opinion/matthew-soerens-jenny-yang-trump-refugees-ronald-reagan.

[3]Matthew Soerens and Jenny Yang, *Welcoming the Stranger* (Downers Grove, IL: InterVarsity Press, 2018).

19. The Happiest Place on Earth

[1]Jamila Reddy, "The Activism of Self-Care: 5 Things to Help You Heal," *Philadelphia Printworks*, December 13, 2016, https://philadelphia-printworks.myshopify.com/blogs/news/the-activism-of-self-care-5-things-to-help-you-heal.

[2]See Eugene Peterson, *A Long Obedience in the Same Direction* (Downers Grove, IL: InterVarsity Press, 2019).

20. Empire

[1]Nick Page, "Exile 79: Exile Stories," *Mid-Faith Crisis*, accessed September 20, 2019, https://midfaithcrisis.org/podcast/episode-79-exile-stories.

[2]James Baldwin, *Notes of a Native Son* (Boston: Beacon Press, 1984), 9.

21. Billboards

[1]Shane Claiborne, Jonathan Wilson-Hartgrove, and Enuma Okoro, *Common Prayer: A Liturgy for Ordinary Radicals* (Grand Rapids, MI: Zondervan, 2015), 555.

[2]Grace Lichtenstein, "Sold Only in the West, Coors Beer Is Smuggled to the East," *New York Times*, December 28, 1975, www.nytimes.com/1975/12/28/archives/article-4-no-title-sold-only-in-the-west-coors-beer-is-smuggled-to.html.

[3]B. Erin Cole and Allyson Brantley, "The Coors Boycott: When a Beer Can Signaled Your Politics," *CPR News*, October 3, 2014, www.cpr.org/2014/10/03/the-coors-boycott-when-a-beer-can-signaled-your-politics.

22. The Pioneer Mind

[1]Louise Erdrich, *The Birchbark House* (New York: HarperCollins, 2008).

[2]See Doug Wilson, a founder of the classical Christian education and his book *Black and Tan* (Moscow, ID: Canon Press, 2005). Here is one quote: "The intellectual leadership of the South was conservative, orthodox, and Christian. In contrast, the leadership of the North was radical and Unitarian. . . . On the slavery issue the drums of war were being beaten by the abolitionists, who in turn were driven by a zealous hatred of the Word of God" (p. 47).

[3]For more information on biblicism and how evangelicals in the United States read the Bible, see Christian Smith, *The Bible Made Impossible: Why Biblicism Is Not a Truly Evangelical Reading of Scripture* (Grand Rapids, MI: Brazos, 2012).

[4]To get a sense of the viewpoints of Bob Jones Sr. himself, consider this: he preached his self-avowed "most important sermon ever" on Easter Sunday 1960 on how segregation was scriptural—and this sermon was given to every student who entered the school from 1960–1986. The BJU campus did not allow interracial

dating until 2000 (and only changed their policy due to public outcry) and African Americans were not admitted until 1971. See Camille Lewis, "'Is Segregation Scriptural?' by Bob Jones SR, 1960," *A Time to Laugh* (blog), March 15, 2013, www.drslewis.org/camille/2013/03/15/is-segregation-scriptural-by-bob-jones-sr-1960 and "History of Bob Jones University," *Wikipedia*, accessed September 23, 2019, https://en.wikipedia.org/wiki/History_of_Bob_Jones_University.

[5]Willie James Jennings, *The Christian Imagination: Theology and the Origins of Race* (New Haven, CT: Yale University Press, 2010), 17.

[6]Jennings, *Christian Imagination*, 22.

[7]Michael R. Lowman and Corinne Sawtelle, *United States History in Christian Perspective: Heritage of Freedom*, 3rd ed. (Pensacola, FL: Abeka Press, 2012), 238.

[8]Lowman and Sawtelle, *United States History in Christian Perspective*, 6.

23. Signposts

[1]See Alan Ehrenhart, *The Great Inversion and the Future of the American City* (New York: Random House, 2012).

[2]For more on this topic, see Mark Charles and Soong-Chan Rah, *Unsettling Truths: The Ongoing, Dehumanizing Legacy of the Doctrine of Discovery* (Downers Grove, IL: InterVarsity Press, 2019).

[3]Nikole Hannah-Jones, "America Wasn't a Democracy, Until Black Americans Made It One," *New York Times*, August 14, 2019, www.nytimes.com/interactive/2019/08/14/magazine/black-history-american-democracy.html.

24. Monuments and Memorials

[1]Matthew Kaemingk, *Christian Hospitality and Muslim Immigration in an Age of Fear* (Grand Rapids, MI: Eerdmans, 2018), 82.

[2]William Stringfellow, *An Ethic for Christians and Other Aliens in a Strange Land* (Eugene, OR: Wipf & Stock, 2004), 85.

[3]For more on his life and work see Bryan Stevenson, *Just Mercy* (New York: Spiegel & Grau, 2015).

[4]Ta-Nehisi Coates, "The Case for Reparations," *Atlantic*, June 22, 2018, www.theatlantic.com/magazine/archive/2014/06/the-case-for-reparations/361631.

25. Learning from Exiles

[1]While there is no direct quote of Lewis here, Sehnsucht was a common theme in his life and writings—see the journal devoted to him and this idea at "Sehnsucht: The C. S. Lewis Journal," *Logos*, accessed September 23, 2019, www.logos.com/product/49483/sehnsucht-the-cs-lewis-journal?.

[2]C. S. Lewis, *The Weight of Glory and Other Addresses* (New York: William Collins, 2013), 30-31.

[3]Lisa Sharon Harper, *The Very Good Gospel* (Colorado Springs, CO: WaterBrook, 2016), 13.

[4]Randy S. Woodley, *Shalom and the Community of Creation: An Indigenous Vision* (Grand Rapids, MI: Eerdmans, 2012), 11.

[5]Ida B. Wells-Barnett, *Southern Horrors: Lynch Law in All Its Phases* (Old Delhi, India: Alpha Editions, 2018), 7.

[6]James H. Cone, *The Cross and the Lynching Tree* (Maryknoll, NY: Orbis Books, 2015), 31. Please read the entire book, with a special emphasis on chapter two and how Reinhold Niebuhr in particular missed the clear connections between the cross and the lynchings of Black men and women in America.

[7]George Tsakiridis, "Vine and Fig Tree," George Washington's Mount Vernon, accessed September 23, 2019, www.mountvernon.org/library/digitalhistory/digital-encyclopedia/article/vine-and-fig-tree.

[8]Randy Woodley, *Shalom and the Community of Creation: an Indigenous Vision* (Grand Rapids, MI: Eerdmans, 2012), 15.

Epilogue

[1]Jesse van Eerdman, *A Sense of Wonder: The World's Best Writers on the Sacred, the Profane, and the Ordinary* (Maryknoll, NY: Orbis Books, 2016).

[2]Walter Brueggemann, *Hopeful Imagination: Prophetic Voices in Exile* (Minneapolis: Fortress Press, 1987), 23-24.